VOICES AGAINST SEX SLAVERY IN AMERICA

Perspectives on Fighting Sex Trafficking

Compiled By

Aayushi Shah and Katie Bemb

Dedicated to those whose voices haven't been heard.

Thanks also to the Rawlings Undergraduate Leadership Fellows Program for inspiring us to unite all of these voices in a project that we hope will encourage a multi-stakeholder approach to combating sex trafficking in America.

VOICES AGAINST SEX SLAVERY IN AMERICA

Perspectives on Fighting Sex Trafficking

Compiled By

Aayushi Shah and Katie Bemb

Bowman Publishing
U.S.A.

VOICES AGAINST SEX SLAVERY IN AMERICA
Perspectives on Fighting Sex Trafficking

ISBN-10: 0-9988869-1-2

ISBN-13: 978-0-9988869-1-6

Printed in the United States of America

A special big thanks to Christopher Weir for designing and creating the book's front and back covers.

The views and opinions expressed in this book are those of the authors and may not necessarily reflect the views and beliefs of Bowman Publishing or of the other co-authors. This book occasionally contains stories of crime and violence (which may be unsuitable for children). Each author has written based upon his or her unique personal experiences. The writings of this book are not produced to condone or glorify crime or violence but to encourage others to avoid being sexually exploited with hopes that this book will inspire people to become vigilant and helpers to others in our communities and around the world

Contents

Foreword...7
Introduction...11

Section I: Government

Deanna Wallace...17
Kate Reilly...23
Thomas Stack...29

Section II: Law

Ayn B. Ducao...37
Elizabeth Landau...41
Shea Rhodes...45

Section III: Nonprofits

Erin Andrews...53
Diane Amos...61
Iona Rudisill...69
Jacquelin Hahn...77
Karen Kutzner...81
Kay Chernush...85
Lawrence Bowman...91
Michele Clark...103
Susan Esserman...109

Section IV: Therapy and Health Care

Dr. Anita Ravi....117
Irene Jacobs....121
Katherine Hargitt....127

Section V: Survivors and Family Members

Craig and Lisa McLaughlin....137
Shayla Davis....143

Section VI: Advocacy

Aubrey Sneesby....149
Emily Long....153
Sarah Lin....157
Youngbee Dale....163

Section VII: Journalism

Lisa Driscoll....169

References and Resources....174

Foreword

Human trafficking involves the exploitation of human beings by human beings. This crime is also known as modern day slavery. While we all learned in our American history classes that slavery was abolished in 1865, a closer look reveals that it still exists. Slavery exists in all countries on all continents, including North America. In fact, all forms of human trafficking, especially sex trafficking, occur in cities across the United States.

Whether the city is Boise, Idaho, or College Park, Maryland, people of all ages and sexualities are being compelled to trade sex for money, drugs or even shelter. These individuals are manipulated by traffickers or pimps. They are made to believe that the exploitation is an act of love. They may even be blackmailed into being raped day after day by strangers, because the traffickers have established the belief that the individuals under their control or even family members will be in danger if the demands are not met with compliance. Sex trafficking in the United States, including domestic minor sex trafficking, can occur at the hands of parents, siblings, neighbors, landlords or even employers.

Aayushi and Katie have decided to shape an academic project into a book that seeks to illuminate stakeholders in the issue of domestic sex trafficking. These two students want the public to know that advocates and adversaries walk among us everyday. Page by page you will learn about the relationships that fuel oppression. Survivors will share their experiences including their triumphs and their heartbreaks. We will learn how they felt walking, shopping, working or even attending school day by day unable to escape the darkness of being trafficked. Activists will share how their efforts contribute to the creation of new laws to protect potential and current victims from future victimization and criminalization. We will learn how these professionals inform the public to allow for more keen understanding of identifiable red flags of potential trafficking situations. The stories will also reveal the high degree of connectivity that exists amongst all of us as related to this issue.

Human trafficking has been at the forefront of conversations and public awareness campaigns for the past two decades, during a time when we thought we were finished with having to figure out why some people in the world were exploiting other people in the world. This book aims to highlight the struggles and the successes in this journey towards again combating and abolishing slavery.

—Dr. Christine White, University of Maryland

&

Dr. Wendy Stickle, University of Maryland

Aayushi Shah
and
Katie Bemb

Introduction

We are junior University of Maryland students partnering on a community action project focused on domestic sex trafficking awareness and education for the Rawlings Undergraduate Leadership Fellows Program. Our project was initially modeled off of Brandon Stanton's "Humans of New York" journalistic social media campaign. We reached out to survivors, family members of survivors, attorneys, journalists, law enforcement, policy makers, scholars and other stakeholders in order to effectively portray the scope of the issue of domestic sex trafficking and how we can begin to reach a solution.

We want to break the myth that sex trafficking is a foreign issue. It occurs right here in America, and our project points to different ways we can combat this illicit trade. Through this book, we hope to provide a more holistic perspective on what human trafficking looks like in America, what is currently being done to combat the issue, and what still needs to be done moving forward.

As many of our contributors emphasized, collaboration is essential. Stakeholders need to coordinate in order to eradicate sex slavery in America. There is no point in reinventing the wheel; many of the tools needed to fight this illicit criminal enterprise already exist.

The first installation of our project was our social media campaign. We reached out to over 300 stakeholders who are connected to anti-trafficking measures and asked them to participate in our social media campaign. The second piece of our project is this book. Our goal is for this book to serve as a resource and to be used in curricula to increase awareness and educate people about the reality of sex trafficking in America. We hope that the passion, dedication, and hard work of our contributors inspires our readers and serves as a call for action.

On the first day of the Rawlings Undergraduate Leadership Fellows Program, all the fellows were asked to introduce themselves and describe an issue that we would work on if we had 24 hours to change the world. We both said we would focus on human trafficking, and in that moment we knew we wanted to work together on our community action project. This whole process has been such an incredible journey for us. We have learned so much, and we have gotten to speak with so many amazing people who are doing valuable work to fight human trafficking in the United States. We hope that our readers will gain as much insight into domestic sex trafficking while reading this book as we did while researching and compiling these contributions.

A little bit about ourselves...

Aayushi Shah is a junior government and politics major with minors in Spanish and technology entrepreneurship. In Spring 2017, she interned with the University of Maryland SAFE Center for human trafficking survivors as the Research and Outreach intern. She is currently a research assistant for the Robert H. Smith School of Business and a Democracy Summer fellow, which is a project created by a congressman from Maryland that introduces students to progressive politics. In fall 2017, she will be entering the Hinman CEOs program, the nation's first living-learning entrepreneurship program, and she will be interning at the United States Attorney's Office in D.C. After her undergraduate career, she plans on going to law school and relentlessly fighting for social justice issues. She looks at law and public policy as means to bring opportunity and justice to society's most underserved and marginalized communities.

Katie Bemb is a junior journalism major and Public Leadership Scholars with a minor in international development and conflict management. In spring 2016, she interned for the School of Public Policy to help plan Climate Action 2016, a multi-stakeholder conference discussing implementation of the Paris Agreement. She has written and edited for a number of campus publications, including The Diamondback, Stories Beneath the Shell, Pulsefeedz, Her Campus and Unwind Magazine. She works for College Park Scholars managing communications and also for University Relations assisting the University of Maryland's development officers. She hopes to utilize her communication skills to enact social change through domestic policy and global human rights development. After achieving her bachelor's degree in journalism, she hopes to obtain a job at a university in the Washington, D.C. area where she can explore both her passion for human rights development and her interest in higher education.

SECTION I

GOVERNMENT

Deanna Wallace
Victim Witness Services
Department of Homeland Security

Deanna Wallace

I started my career as victim advocate at a local sexual assault agency as an intern. I never thought this would be my career, and I couldn't have imagined where being a victim advocate would take me. After I graduated college I worked as an in-home counselor, which was hard for me because we were more like a required check-in-the box rather than people who could actually assist. Subsequently, I went to work within the criminal justice system as director of a victim witness program, then as victim witness coordinator. I thought I had an idea of trauma and its effect on people. I was wrong. I learned that not everyone wants to be rescued, and even with protection in place, people are not always protected.

After serving as a victim witness coordinator for over three years, I went to work for the Marine Corps. My spouse and I retired from the Army almost 29 years ago. When I saw there was a need for victim advocates, I jumped at the chance. Little did I realize that I would not only work with domestic violence and sexual assault victims, but I would also meet my first sex trafficking victim.

I was briefed on a domestic violence case that was marked as strange, and the command was worried about the victim. She was young, developmentally delayed and had just had a baby. That was all I learned about the case. After my first meeting with her I knew there was something deeper, so I requested a meeting with the case manager. She explained more about the case and gave me more facts of the abuse. The husband didn't physically harm her himself, but we knew that this case involved more than emotional abuse.

After doing some digging, we learned that this husband was forcing his young bride to drive to the base and wait in the car until johns came with money to have sex with her while their young daughter was in the vehicle. I honestly can't say what horrified me more: that an active duty Marine husband would care so little about his wife and daughter or that men would pay to have sex with a young mom while her daughter was in the car.

I did the only thing I knew to do. I worked the case like we were trained. I made sure the bad guy was away from the victim and then stabilized her and her daughter. Done. He was locked up in the brig and she had no contact with him. What we didn't think to look further into was the trafficking aspect. We didn't mention, and really didn't even know, that we had just worked a sex trafficking case. In this case, the young victim had so many issues that stabilization was hard enough for us. I can't even imagine what I would have done for her if I had understood that she was a victim of trafficking. That case stayed with me and made me question who she was and what the case was really about. I read as much as I could about trafficking and what I needed to do better for the next victim. When I saw that Homeland Security Investigations was hiring, I jumped at the chance to learn more about the crime of trafficking and what I could do for more trafficking victims.

Even after having seen all that I had, I don't think I was prepared for working with these victims. I say victim and not survivor because when you work in the justice system, you are not supposed to call them survivors. If you live through a car accident, then you survived the accident. If all of your family is killed, then you are the lone survivor. But if you are talking about domestic violence, sexual assault, child abuse or human trafficking, you are a victim of the crime according to the justice system. Otherwise, you are the defendant or a witness to the crime. Despite the professional terminology, I fully embrace using the term 'survivor,' and hope that I can explain that well enough to my victims. I say 'victim' so that other professionals recognize the rights that are afforded to victims of crime. Witnesses don't have rights and don't have a say in the system. But a victim has rights that must be given to them by federal and state government officials.

I am hopeful for an increase in recognition of the fact that sex trafficking happens everywhere. I hope for the sake of victims that we continually change and evolve within the justice system. I know it must feel like change is so slow, but we have to remember how few rights, protections and resources sex trafficking victims had in the 1980s. Those victims and victim advocates paved the way for us now. They fought every day to make sure people were safe and that victims' voices were heard. I started working for HSI in 2013 when Virginia had no trafficking laws; we got our sex trafficking laws in 2015. Before these laws were in place, human trafficking cases were sent to a federal court. So, that change is huge! We are currently working on labor trafficking laws.

The next question is even more important. What can we do better? (You shouldn't ask that question to a victim assistance specialist.)

I recently spoke to a victim (she made sure to correct me that she is a survivor) and we talked about what we need to do better. She wanted me to talk about how entering prostitution is not the beginning of the cycle, but merely part of it. This begs a number of questions: When do people learn about trafficking? When would someone become vulnerable to trafficking? Is it when they are approached by a trafficker? Or is it the first time they hear a song or see a photo of trafficking? What about watching a movie dedicated to making trafficking look glamorous?

What would that introduction look like and sound like? In reality, the first time a child is introduced to trafficking is through Hollywood and social media. In my perfect world there would not be a foundation laid that traffickers can build upon. Songs, movies and television glamorize trafficking. Have you noticed? If you want to make something bigger and cooler, what would you call it? Would you call it pimpin'?

If you search the internet and type in "Pimp my…" you will be surprised what pops up. When did it become OK to say "Pimp my child?" When did we start to look at pimping as something that is desirable?

We glamorize pimps and give them celebrity status. Pimps exploit and abuse women. What kind of cultural shift enables 'pimp' to evolve into an acceptable, and even complimentary, word? How can we change people's opinions on what trafficking really is?

We first need to understand that there are still people who won't acknowledge the difference between prostitution and trafficking. If we want to learn about trafficking but still don't understand the difference, how can we expect that the victims will? If children and teens are exposed to trafficking as something that is to be desired, then we have already failed. If they are approached by a trafficker, they could be curious and willing to speak with them. They have already seen the images of the money and glamor that are associated with trafficking. They have heard songs about how it's all about respect and making money. These images show victims with money all over them; they show smiling faces and how others aspire to be like them.

What they don't show is the terror and brutality of the

crime, the forced drug usage and rapes. How do we challenge these images and misconceptions? By working on laws that protect our victims after we identify them and working with amazing nonprofits that work tirelessly for survivors. Unfortunately, this won't automatically change society's idea of trafficking. We need to work on adding layers of protection to the victim *before* they see a photo or watch a movie that glamorizes pimps and prostitution. Remind your friends and family of the difference between a prostitute and a trafficking victim; this is the difference between a criminal and a victim. Ask yourself whether all prostitutes really want to be doing what they are doing.

How can we get TV shows to talk about sex trafficking rings instead of prostitution rings? If the show or news story call describes a mom or dad selling their child to traffickers, this needs to be clearly designated as sex trafficking, not child prostitution. If you hear a song that talks about how women are whores, don't just ignore it. We have used words that have promoted trafficking for long enough in our society. We have shamed and disrespected these survivors long enough. If you think that words can't hurt, you haven't spoken with a victim or survivor of sex trafficking.

Kate Reilly, Special Agent
U.S. Department of Homeland Security
HSI New Orleans - Human Trafficking and Child Recovery Task Force

Kate Reilly

Working human trafficking investigations began for me right out of the training academy in 2009 when I arrived at the Baltimore Field Office. It was not the program area that I was permanently assigned to, but we had a large juvenile sex trafficking case that needed the assistance of every agent in the unit.

Although I had been taught in the academy about the definition of human trafficking, I had no idea what that really meant until I arrived in the field office. I can still remember the first time I looked at the escorts section on *Backpage.com*; I was absolutely floored. I had no idea that website existed, let alone that it was a place for pimps to prostitute juveniles. I was eventually permanently assigned to investigate human trafficking cases.

I spent my first two years in human trafficking investigations learning as much as I could from two great field training agents, as well as many state and local investigators who had been doing these cases for years. These agents and investigators were all very different, but I gleaned a tremendous amount of information and experience from them, not just about investigating human trafficking, but also about being a good agent. I assisted on all kinds of cases, including domestic sex trafficking, massage parlors, brothels and labor trafficking. This time was invaluable for me as I really honed my interview skills.

During this time, one of my training agents asked if I believed in victims. I wasn't really sure what he meant, but before I could respond he said, "There are victims of human trafficking and it may not seem like they are victims, but they are." As the rookie, you just nod and say OK, but it quickly became apparent what he meant. Over the last seven years I have recovered and interviewed hundreds of adult and child trafficking victims. Every time I sit down with a victim I have to remind myself of what my training agent said. Most of these men, women or children do not see themselves as being exploited or victimized. It is our job to recognize and understand that in order to elicit the information during an interview and, ultimately, build a case. This can be extremely difficult since these victims have so many barriers built up from the years of physical, sexual and emotional abuse. So, it can often be an ongoing process to earn their trust and get the whole story.

In 2014, I transferred to the New Orleans Field Office. After just a few weeks, two things became immediately clear to me: 1) there was a tremendous lack of law enforcement personnel dedicated to working human trafficking, and 2) there were very minimal proactive efforts aimed at recovering juveniles. One of the first cases I worked involved a 3-year-old who was being groomed for prostitution. After working that case, I was on a mission to implement more proactive measures in combating child sex trafficking and to dedicate more resources to the issue. Now, two years later, we have developed a team of investigators from different federal, state and local agencies who assist with recovering child victims of sex trafficking and charging those responsible for their exploitation. The results of these efforts have exceeded all my expectations. It really shows what can happen when people who genuinely care about helping these kids come together to make a difference. The efforts of this team are only continuing to grow and expand; I can't wait to see what is accomplished in another two years.

I think going forward it is important for our society as a whole to take better care of our children and provide them with good role models. No child at the age of 13 or 14 should ever feel that his or her best option is to get involved in prostitution. We also need to get more involved with the families, schools and community organizations by raising awareness about the signs and indicators of children at risk for trafficking. Parents today need to be vigilant, observant, and not afraid to ask their children questions about their activities, friends and associates. Most importantly, we must encourage parents, relatives and guardians to contact law enforcement and/or service providers for assistance as soon as possible if they suspect a child is in danger or at-risk for trafficking.

I would also like to see lawmakers and celebrity advocates working more closely with law enforcement on this issue. I so often see decisions being made and programs being implemented that are actually harming our investigative efforts. I urge those with a public voice who have an interest in this area to reach out to law enforcement on the ground level. This is the only way to gain a true perspective on what's really happening (or not happening) when it comes to combating human trafficking. It is not enough to just identify and recover the victims. I firmly believe that one of the most effective ways to end trafficking is to hold those accountable who exploit and sell other human beings. In many states in this country, the bond amounts, sentencing and actual time served on these cases is embarrassing. It is also a hindrance to getting victim/witness cooperation. Multiple times I've heard a victim say, "What's the point of talking to you, when my pimp is going to be out on bond in a couple weeks? He will know I talked and he will kill me." It's only when the punishment outweighs the benefit of committing the crime that we will start to see the problem curtailed.

I've been working these cases for over seven years now, and I consider myself blessed because I have the unique opportunity to go out every single day and potentially help a child get out of a life of prostitution. Not many people can say that, which is what makes it such a powerful experience. Oftentimes, we are the only people besides the pimp who have taken an interest in that child. Although they don't typically show it at the time we recover them, children often tell me later on that they were happy or relieved we came to find them.

Unfortunately, I think being a human trafficking investigator is one of the most thankless jobs in law enforcement. The burnout rate is high and it is generally frowned upon by other officers and investigators as not being real police work. Despite all of that, I still love what I do because every so often I get a text from a survivor or a parent thanking me for what I did and telling me all the good things that have happened in their life since I intervened. It's those rare and precious words that make all the days, months and years of hard work worth it.

Thomas Stack
Public Safety Policy Analyst
Governor's Office of Crime Control & Prevention

Thomas Stack

As the public safety policy analyst for the Governor's Office of Crime Control and Prevention, I coordinate statewide efforts to combat human trafficking in Maryland. Prior to this role, I served as a police detective with the Montgomery County Department of Police. With over 14 years of experience with human trafficking, I have unfortunately seen this lucrative criminal enterprise grow significantly.

In 2001, I was transferred from a very proactive street crimes unit to a slower paced vice and intelligence unit which captured more intelligence than vice work (e.g. prostitution and gambling). At that time, the term 'human trafficking' was unheard of and, for the most part, prostitution was not really investigated. In fact, human trafficking was viewed by many as a victimless crime or just a nuisance crime. Once I entered the vice and intelligence unit, I started investigating vice-related crimes in massage parlors in Montgomery County. During this time, the Montgomery County police department was still unaware of any human trafficking situations, and therefore, no training efforts or guidance on how to speak with the women in massage parlors occurred. Later, in 2003, Montgomery County witnessed an increase in the number of Latino brothels. I then focused my attention on this emerging problem, despite the lack of training specific to human trafficking.

Upon entering my first Latino brothel, I could immediately tell that the women inside did not choose to be there. The language barriers and cultural differences made it very difficult for me to talk to these women and ask if they needed help. In March 2005, I attended my first human trafficking training, after which I began to view things differently. I started to look at every case assigned to me as a possible human trafficking case. Of the vast majority of possible victims encountered, only a few ever asked for help. This became very frustrating, because I knew that these women needed help. I became even more determined to find some way to reach each of them.

Around 2006 the internet became the most popular place for traffickers to advertise for prostitution. Montgomery County had never had a place for street prostitution, and most of the domestic prostitution occurred in Washington, D.C., or a few underground advertisements in the city paper or Yellow Pages. The internet changed everything, and the lower-end hotels in the county started to fill up. I began to see that the domestic victims of human trafficking far outnumbered the international victims. I started seeing the pimp in a new light, and thought that the media hype and glorification of these pimps was shameful. I realized that my unit was in no position to help any victim by themselves, so I began to align myself with trusted service providers, such as Polaris Project, Courtney's House and TurnAround, Inc.

I treated every sting operation as a possible human trafficking case and gave every girl the chance to escape that life without the fear of arrest. My focus became on the trafficker and not the trafficked and, as a result, I was able to refer several women to service providers. The only thing more rewarding than arresting a trafficker was to see a victim of trafficking get her life back. In one case my unit was conducting a sting operation at a hotel in Rockville, Maryland, where I entered a room and began talking to the female who told me her name. We will call her 'K.' I offered my assistance to help get her out of this life, and she told me that she was tired and needed my help. Even though I had more than enough evidence to arrest her and charge her with prostitution, that was not my goal. More important than making an arrest was helping K get her life back. I introduced K to staff at a Maryland service provider who started to work with her. Ms. Melissa Snow and Ms. Amelia Rubenstein worked with K for four years to help restore her life. I occasionally see K, who is now doing great, raising her family and working full time.

I started to notice how young many of these girls were, and I began to focus my attention on child sex trafficking victims. I devised my own method of searching the internet to look for children who were being prostituted online. Since the FBI Baltimore Field Office did not have a Child Exploitation Task Force at the time, I started working with the FBI out of the Washington Field Office. There we began exchanging information on runaways, and I built a solid working relationship with the agents and the analyst. This partnership paid off with my first federal child sex trafficking case in 2007. The trafficker received a 10-year prison sentence in that case for trafficking a 16-year-old runaway who I recovered in Montgomery County.

Around 2008, people started asking me to provide trainings and presentations for various stakeholders to include law enforcement and citizen groups in combating human trafficking. As a result, I developed a passion for sharing my expertise with others, and was fortunate enough to travel to Russia, El Salvador, Thailand and all over the United States, teaching about human trafficking investigations. In 2010, I was the first task force officer of the newly formed FBI Maryland Child Exploitation Task Force. Through this task force I forged many long lasting professional relationships that still exist today. I started the investigation into a violent trafficker that led to a 36-year federal prison sentence. Jeremy Naughton was a violent trafficker (pimp) from Brooklyn, New York. Mr. Naughton would kidnap, beat and traffick his victims from New York to Maryland. This *United States v. Jeremy Naughton* case is one of the highlights of my law enforcement career.

I retired from law enforcement in September 2014; however, I wanted to continue my work to stop human trafficking. I wanted to continue teaching law enforcement how to identify and investigate human trafficking cases. Even though I was no longer in a position to recover victims, I wanted to show others the importance of a victim-centered approach to trafficking.

In May 2015, I was hired as the human trafficking policy analyst for the Governor's Office of Crime Control and Prevention. As a result, I have made law enforcement training a priority, and I want to see that every law enforcement officer in the State of Maryland receives human trafficking training. With the assistance of the United States Attorney's Office, I have trained over 1,300 officers in my current role and have seen the number of victims identified increase in the locations where the trainings were given. I am a member of, and coordinate with, the Maryland Safe Harbor Workgroup, which was formed by legislation and directed to study legal protections for youth victims of human trafficking, the provision of services for youth victims of human trafficking and to report its findings and recommendations to the governor and General Assembly.

While anti-human trafficking efforts have come a long way since 2001, there is much work that still needs to be done. Fortunately, human trafficking now has the attention of many, including police officers, community leaders and legislators. Legislators are especially important as they have the power to strengthen laws to help victims of trafficking take back their lives and hold traffickers responsible. My only regret so far is that I was unable to rescue every victim of human trafficking that I came in contact with, but I am hopeful that, with the increased understanding and commitment to this problem in the future, together we can help all victims.

SECTION II

LAW

Ayn B. Ducao
Assistant Attorney
U.S. Attorney's Office, Maryland

Ayn B. Ducao

Since summer 2015, I have served as the human trafficking coordinator for the U.S. Attorney's Office and, in that capacity, I serve as the chairperson of the Maryland Human Trafficking Task Force (MHTTF). The goal of the task force is to work collaboratively with state, federal and private agencies and organizations to identify and restore victims of human trafficking while investigating and prosecuting offenders. Members of the task force include partners from state and local law enforcement and prosecutors, victim service providers, non-governmental organizations, and many other entities.

With regard to sex trafficking under federal law, the primary statute is 18 U.S.C. § 1591, which is a felony that relates to sex trafficking of a minor, or trafficking by force, fraud or coercion. If a minor is trafficked, 18 U.S.C. § 1591 provides for a mandatory minimum of 10 years imprisonment and maximum sentence of life. If force, fraud or coercion is used – regardless of whether the victim is a minor – the mandatory minimum is 10 years imprisonment and maximum sentence of life.

My own cases have primarily centered around child sex trafficking, with victims primarily ranging from 14 to 17 years old. I believe that to successfully prosecute these cases requires a multidisciplinary approach, or to steal a famous phrase, it takes a village. A multidisciplinary approach involves prosecutors, law enforcement and victims' services, including social services and child protective services. It requires trying to address all of the needs of the victims, who are often vulnerable and have suffered profound trauma.

These cases are among the most difficult but also the most rewarding that I have prosecuted. Human trafficking cases are difficult cases, in that they are very labor- and resource-intensive and usually require collaboration between all involved partners, including prosecutors, law enforcement and victim services. The victims of human trafficking may find it difficult to trust law enforcement and prosecutors, and therefore may be reluctant to assist in a prosecution. Building trust with a victim is thus a process that can take a great deal of time. In addition, while law enforcement tries to find evidence to corroborate the testimony of the victims, sometimes there are facts and testimonies that only the victims can provide and it becomes a credibility determination for the jury. It is also difficult because juries (and judges) may not see a sex trafficking survivor as a person who was victimized, but rather as a person who consented to being trafficked. If one has not personally encountered instances of trauma bonding, it can be difficult for ordinary citizens to understand the complex relationships between traffickers and their victims. For example, so-called

"Romeo pimps" use seemingly romantic and sexual relationships and other more subtle pressures to get their victims to engage in commercial sex acts.

However, these cases are also incredibly rewarding, because you get to advocate for victims who need persons who can stand up for them and help them move on with their lives. I recently learned that a 14-year-old victim from a case I prosecuted a few years ago is now potentially college-bound. A 16-year-old victim from a case that I recently tried has told me that she wants to join the armed forces and become a doctor. Even getting these victims to consider such future plans for their lives would not be possible if they were still being trafficked.

What I would like to see more broadly is an education campaign similar to the ones that advocates for victims of domestic abuse have been waging for years to shift the focus from "why does she stay" to "why doesn't he leave and what he did was illegal." Victims of human trafficking, especially child victims, do not and cannot give real consent to be trafficked and I hope that the public will become better educated to that fact.

Elizabeth Landau
Staff Attorney
Amara Legal Center

Elizabeth Landau

My first misconception about human trafficking was that it existed somewhere else. My second misconception about human trafficking was that it only happened to certain types of people. Imagine my surprise when I met a trafficking survivor who lived in my city and graduated from the same college I was attending.

I grew up in a small suburb outside of Kansas City. In my mind, I had a normal childhood, went to a normal school and had a normal family. I read stories about things that happened in other places, but I did not see those things around me in the day to day. I was oblivious, and it wasn't until I began an internship in college at an anti-trafficking organization that I realized the extent of the issue. It was shocking to meet so many people from my area that had been trafficked. This was not an issue occurring overseas; it was happening all around me.

So many of these harmful practices are hidden, difficult to spot, and often shielded by systems intending to help. It was shocking to discover how easy it is to fall into them. A few months unemployment could lead to homelessness. An overwhelming amount of stressful circumstances, out of your control, could lead to mental health issues. An adult figure you trust could abuse your relationship and usher you into trafficking. While I felt that I had control over my life, I realized how many circumstances were not in my control. Many things in my life were a result of luck or happenstance. Had the circumstances outside of my control been different, this could have been me. The divide between myself and this survivor no longer existed. The barrier I had created to make myself feel safe evaporated. Her problem became my problem. The logical next step was, what am I going to do about it?

As an attorney, I often work with clients to overcome difficult legal hurdles. I approach it as a team effort, two people working together to achieve results. It is not about saving them. It is not about exploiting their story. It is about empowering and supporting them. There is no such thing as an ideal trafficking victim. Many victims have experienced severe psychological abuse, and they may return to their traffickers several times or have engaged in 'survival sex,' the exchange of sex for money by individuals who cannot find any other way to support themselves. Some of my clients have been rejected by some within the anti-trafficking community because they do not meet that idealized standard. My highest priority is to meet my clients where they are, with their actual experiences, regardless of where he or she may be in the recovery process.

Shea Rhodes
Co-founder and Director
Commercial Sexual Exploitation Institute

Shea Rhodes

I am a co-founder and the director of the Villanova University Charles Widger School of Law Institute to Address Commercial Sexual Exploitation. The CSE Institute's purpose is to educate and provide technical assistance to stakeholders and those who respond to commercial sexual exploitation worldwide, while promoting victim-centered, trauma-informed multidisciplinary collaboration. We equip policymakers and the broader community with the skills and knowledge necessary to improve the legal system's response to commercial sexual exploitation, in order to support survivors and hold perpetrators accountable. In each of our efforts, we center the experiences of survivors, and we are committed to engaging the survivor community in shaping our positions.

I first became aware of the issue of commercial sexual exploitation and domestic sex trafficking when I was working as an assistant district attorney in Philadelphia. As a prosecutor, I understood my job was to faithfully uphold and execute the laws of the Commonwealth of Pennsylvania, in furtherance of my greater duty: to effectuate justice. I was also responsible for keeping the community safe, and I believed the community included offenders as well.

The foundation of the United States criminal justice system is supported by numerous theories, including theories of punishment. A popular theory of punishment is deterrence. The rationale of deterrence is two-fold: Fear of punishment alone will prevent some people from committing crimes, and fear of a harsher punishment will prevent others from becoming repeat or habitual offenders.

In state and federal crimes codes, the theory of deterrence can be implemented simply by increasing the severity of penalties, or offense grading, in correlation with the number of times a specific crime has been committed by the same individual. This is known as the concept of recidivism. For example, in Pennsylvania, the crime of prostitution, whether selling sex or buying sex, (18 Pa.C.S. § 5902(a) and (e) respectively) is a recidivist crime. For first- and second-time offenders, prostitution is graded as a misdemeanor of the third degree (M3). Every crime graded M3 in Pennsylvania's crimes code carries the same maximum sentence: one year in jail and up to $2,500 in fines. For third time offenders, prostitution is graded as misdemeanor of the second degree (M2). In Pennsylvania, those convicted of an M2 crime can be sentenced to two years in prison and up to $5,000 in fines. On the fourth and subsequent offense, the offender is charged with a misdemeanor of the first degree (M1) and faces five years in prison and up to $10,000 in fines.

As assistant district attorney, I was assigned to the

Majors Unit of the Trial Division where I prosecuted violent and complex crimes including carjackings, shootings and home invasions. Throughout my almost 10-year career as a prosecutor, I encountered hundreds of women charged with selling sex, the majority of whom already had four or more convictions for prostitution. I always wondered why we were expending our resources on arresting, charging and convicting women for prostitution, because the threat of recidivist penalties was clearly not acting as a deterrent and the women were clearly being victimized while engaging in selling sex.

After spending close to eight years in the Trial Division, I was given the opportunity to develop policies and protocols for alternative ways to handle cases. In the criminal justice system there are other avenues to resolve criminal cases, such as diversion programs. Diversion programs, or problem-solving courts, acknowledge that the typical court process is not the most beneficial or productive means of effectuating justice for some crimes and for some offender populations. Part of my assignment was to look at cases involving women who had multiple convictions for selling sex and determine whether a diversion program could benefit them, our courts and Philadelphia as a whole.

A pilot program was started in 2010. At first, the process was very ad hoc, with no real structure other than a goal to disrupt the cycle of prostitution arrests. I worked alongside attorneys with the Philadelphia Defender Association and adult probation to develop the specifics of the court program, including participant eligibility, length of the program, and legal benefits and consequences. A Memorandum of Understanding between the Philadelphia courts, District Attorney's Office, Defender Association of Philadelphia, Adult Probation and Parole Department, the Department of Behavioral Health and Intellectual Disability Services and Public Health Management was drafted and signed. Ultimately, Project Dawn Court took shape, and today Project Dawn Court has served over 138 prostituted women.

I am very proud we have a prostitution court diversion program in Philadelphia, although our approach to addressing prostitution is still far from ideal. Most importantly, to have access to a supportive program like Project Dawn Court, a prostituted woman must have at least three prior convictions for prostitution to bring her open case to the necessary misdemeanor of the first degree level. Each prior conviction is a barrier to opportunity and a reinforcement of criminality for prostituted people. Yet, when one considers the realities of a prostituted person, one understands why there is no use for deterrence. Often times, women will engage in prostitution for basic needs and survival. Throughout my career, the overwhelming majority of prostituted people I have encountered are drug-addicted, homeless, or both. They are not criminals. They are not even perpetrators. Rather, they are vulnerable people being victimized and exploited by traffickers and sex buyers.

We need criminal justice reform to address the realities of commercial sexual exploitation. There is inequality in the ways laws related to commercial sex are written, implemented, prosecuted and reported. Consider Pennsylvania's prostitution statute as an example. The law is divided into five substantive subsections — (a), (b), (c), (d), and (e) — of which only sections (a) and (e) recidivise. Though I have been known to joke that law enforcement seemingly forgets to read past section (a), the data is serious:

Again, §5902(a) is simply titled "prostitution," but to be precise the elements of the crime refer to the act of selling sex. Next, the elements of §5902(b) and (b.1), titled "promoting prostitution" and "promoting prostitution of minors" respectfully, connote the acts of pimping or sex trafficking. The following section provides the grading for §5902(b). Then, the next "prostitution" crime is titled "living off prostitutes," and prohibits a person from being financially supported by the proceeds of prostitution. Finally, the last section of the prostitution statute, §5902(e), called "patronizing prostitutes," essentially prohibits a person from purchasing sexual activity from a prostitute "or any other person."

The structure and language of this statute perpetuates stereotypes and promotes misunderstandings about commercial sex and prostituted people in particular. For instance, to include all of these crimes — which arguably have vastly different levels of culpability — in the same section of the crimes code diminishes the exploitation inherent in the act of buying another human being for sexual gratification. Furthermore, the use of the term "prostitute" reinforces the notion that women who sell sex are inferior to the rest of society. "Prostitute" is nothing but a rhetorical barrier to thinking about and treating prostituted women like equal human beings. This point is further exacerbated by the final section of the statute which unmistakably distinguishes between buying sex from a "prostitute" and buying sex from "any other person," as if there was a difference.

Making amendments to the Pennsylvania state prostitution statute would undoubtedly inspire positive change and possibly reduce incidents of commercial sexual exploitation. That is, the law would target the true perpetrators (i.e. pimps and sex buyers) and deterrence would be an effective way to stop sex buyers from repeating their crimes. However, it is not enough to simply change the law on paper, we must change the perceptions of those who enforce the laws and the perception of society at large to truly and justly make sustainable change worthy to honor all victims and survivors of commercial sexual exploitation and sex trafficking. I look forward to continuing the fight.

SECTION III

NONPROFITS

Erin Andrews
Director of Policy
FAIR Girls

Erin Andrews

My name is Erin Andrews, and I am the Director of Policy at FAIR Girls. FAIR Girls is a non-profit organization, established in 2004 and headquartered in Washington, D.C., that serves young women and girls aged 11 to 26 who have escaped all forms of human trafficking. FAIR stands for Free, Aware, Inspired and Restored, as these are some of the things we help victims achieve as they try to leave behind the shackles of human trafficking.

FAIR Girls has served more than 1,000 survivors, 90 percent of whom are American citizens from a wide range of backgrounds. In 2013, FAIR Girls opened the Vida Home, a 90-day safe home for young women survivors of trafficking ages 17 to 26. It is currently the only home of its type in Washington, D.C., that provides emergency housing to this age range of trafficking survivors. FAIR Girls offers counseling, direct services, emergency care, job and educational assistance, and court advocacy. In 2016, FAIR Girls launched Solaine, the policy branch of FAIR Girls, whose mission is to promote critical legislative initiatives, policies and laws, both locally and nationally, that are informed by and rooted in the experiences of the survivors we serve.

I came to FAIR Girls from a law enforcement background. I was an assistant United States attorney at the United States Attorney's Office for the District of Columbia ("USAO-DC") for seven years, where I investigated and prosecuted an array of crimes in the United States District Court for the District of Columbia and the Superior Court for the District of Columbia. As an AUSA, I successfully managed federal and local prosecutions of multiple defendants for sex trafficking of minors and obstruction of justice; obtained convictions in cold cases involving prolonged child sexual abuse and incest; investigated multiple sexual assault cases involving adults and minors employing the collection, analysis, and use of forensic DNA evidence, including the Combined DNA Index System (CODIS); investigated sex offender registration violations on the federal and local level; tried dozens of cases involving intra-family violence; and presented case studies to the human trafficking task force to further the multidisciplinary approach to the prosecution of adult and child trafficking cases.

Prior to working at the USAO-DC, I was an associate at Williams & Connolly LLP for several years after graduating from Georgetown University Law Center, where I was a member of the Domestic Violence Clinic. However, my passion for working on violence against women issues, including domestic violence and human trafficking, reaches all the way back to my days as an undergraduate student at The University of Notre Dame where I studied psychology, sociology, gender studies, and the interplay of those disciplines in the context of the criminal justice system.

I have been humbled by working with victims of human trafficking. I have been inspired. I have learned a great many lessons about the realities of human trafficking. I wanted to share some of those truths here.

I have learned that a lack of opportunities leaves many girls and young women in our communities susceptible to falling prey to traffickers. Traffickers are often cunning and experienced in finding victims who are vulnerable and exploiting that vulnerability in order to lure them into a life of trafficking. The vulnerabilities traffickers exploit are as varied as the girls and young women themselves, ranging from homelessness to loneliness. Understanding this exploitative grooming process is key to understanding so many aspects of the human trafficking epidemic in this country, including how best to empower victims to escape and stay free, and the most effective way to prosecute human trafficking cases.

I have learned that sex trafficking is serial rape for profit. I have seen its depravity. It exists as a criminal enterprise with the trafficker protecting himself from criminal liability on the backs of his victims. I have seen evidence and heard survivor stories of the unimaginable physical, psychological and emotional abuse that traffickers inflict on their victims.

I have learned that there is no such thing as the "perfect" victim. Law enforcement, prosecutors, judges, juries, legislators and society in general have preconceived notions of what a human trafficking victim looks like and acts like. Those preconceptions all too often cloud our ability to recognize victims and treat them as such. I have learned that what further complicates this fact is that human trafficking victims often do not self-identify as victims. Some victims feel so ashamed of what they have been forced to do by their traffickers that they do not want to tell anyone. Some victims have trauma-bonded to their traffickers and consider them the only family they have. Some victims have been coerced or threatened by their traffickers into believing that nobody will believe them or that they or their families will be killed if they talk to law enforcement.

I have learned that survival comes in many forms. What a trafficker forces a victim to do to herself and others should be an opportunity for empathy, not judgment. I have learned that the line between victim and perpetrator is almost never clear and always complicated, and making that determination is one of the hardest things prosecutors investigating these cases do. I have learned that sometimes we get it wrong.

I have learned that the only way to effectively combat human trafficking is from a victim-centered, trauma-informed, multidisciplinary approach, where victims are treated as victims, not criminals, and provided desperately needed resources to begin to stabilize their lives. I have learned that freedom is only the first step in a very long road to recovery for a trafficking victim. Only when we provide human trafficking victims with the resources necessary to heal can they begin the work to escape the cycle of being a vulnerable target for traffickers. Most human trafficking victims want to escape their slavery, even if it does not look like it from the outside, but they have no realistic or safe avenues for doing so. Convictions for crimes committed while being trafficked, homelessness, joblessness, lack of education, immigration concerns and abusive family and foster care situations are insurmountable barriers for these victims.

I have learned that when victims are arrested and charged like criminals in order to leverage cooperation against their traffickers, they are more likely to be uncooperative. I have learned that this strategy of prosecuting human trafficking victims is ineffective, unproductive and fundamentally misunderstands the complexities and realities of human trafficking. I have learned that if any real progress is to be made in successfully prosecuting human trafficking cases it is essential that we stop re-victimizing the victims and find better ways to hold the actual traffickers accountable.

I have learned that our law enforcement partners are working hard every day, and yet human trafficking continues rampantly in our communities. They need to be better equipped with specialized, survivor-informed human trafficking training and strong partnerships with the advocate community and governmental agencies to help them better identify and combat human trafficking. We need to help them do the jobs we have asked them to do.

I have learned that children as young as 11 years old are trafficked or have friends who are being groomed to be trafficked. I have learned that having mandatory violence prevention training that teaches school-age girls and boys about dating violence, sexual abuse and the warning signs of trafficking will give them tools to help keep them safe from trafficking.

I have learned perseverance and restoration is a process that comes in all different forms, but is often cyclical and fraught with setbacks. Some victims flourish when they escape and some founder under the pressures and are forced to return to the cycle of exploitation. However, one of the most hopeful lessons I have learned is that even though the process is long and full of challenges, victims who are connected to resources have a much better chance of making the healing transition from vulnerable victim to survivor.

Lastly, I have learned that we have come a long way in raising awareness, in identifying victims and in forming task-forces to work collaboratively, but we still have a long way to go to end this scourge of modern day slavery. My hope is that by sharing these hard lessons learned with others that we can avoid some of the pitfalls of the past and move towards the policies and programs that will effectively combat human trafficking.

Diane Amos
Director
Free NOLA

Diane Amos

Free NOLA exists to bring hope, love, compassion and restoration to those who perhaps in the eyes of society don't deserve it. One of the most important factors to remember is that human sex trafficking happens everywhere: in your town, your neighborhood and even in your family. No place is sacred and no place is off limits. The only way not to see it is to not look for it.

We first became aware of the atrocities of domestic human sex trafficking during a conference sponsored by the U.S. government in early 2009. The conference (which was held locally) became the awakening we needed to realize that this truly is a domestic problem. Hearing from victims, victim advocates, law enforcement and counselors alike, it was obvious to us that a horrendous crime against humanity was indeed on our own soil, the land of the free. As it is often termed, modern day slavery does exist and it is a reality we must address. However, it wasn't until the 2013 Super Bowl in New Orleans that many of us were able to grasp the gravity and learn the complexities of being caught in the web of the underground sex economy.

Since we deal mostly with women and children, because they make up 73 percent of those identified in the sex industry, we are able to get to the very essence of what women and girls want. In general, they desire to be loved and nurtured, no strings attached. Love is something that most of them do not experience in their formative years — not from their mother, father, relatives, friends, neighbors or even boyfriends.

Without really knowing what or how Free NOLA would deal with the issue, we began doing what seemed natural to us. We reached out to those working in the sex industry with gifts of genuine love, not expecting anything in return. Our goal soon became to show love in a way that could reach the very core of those entrapped. Most working in the industry do not even know that they are being controlled and manipulated; to them it is normal. As many of you know, Bourbon Street is world-renowned for girls and sex. That is where our main focus began. Bourbon Street is our red light district, much like in Amsterdam. Men travel from all over the world to experience what Bourbon Street has to offer.

Since we were new to this type of outreach, we wanted to offer something that spoke to their very hearts. That is the message that we still use today, attached to every gift of love that we offer. The card attached to the gift simply says, "This is a free gift, no strings attached. We just want you to know you are valued, loved and cherished. Should you need any help, don't hesitate to contact us." Of course the reverse side has all the contact information, not an 800 number but my personal contact information. This gives them a level of confidence to know we are not law enforcement or someone who is going to hurt them.

One of the keys to our success is consistency. When someone says they are going to do something for you and then doesn't, this breeds fear and a lack of trust. Pimps do this all the time: They tell the young girl how much they love them, and bring them false hope of glamour, family or relationship. Then bam, they turn the tables on their prey. Now they have them right where they want them: vulnerable, afraid, confused and not able to process what just happened. Once a pimp has gained control of his victim, he can control their body, mind and soul. As a safety measure, the victim will compartmentalize that aspect of their very existence; this is their coping mechanism. As a result, victims shut out the very people who could help them. We come in, not with expectations but with towel in hand (so to speak) to offer kindness, hope and a love that most have never seen before. In other words, we are seed planters, planting seeds of hope and not despair, seeds of love and not condemnation. It is amazing how far one can travel if someone believes in them. Many of these women have children with absentee fathers. Often without education or necessary life skills, many end up on the streets with nowhere to turn. In desperation they turn to the one thing they can do: sell their bodies. But many do not realize that they are also selling their souls. Our job is to come alongside them, encourage them, help them out of the pit they are in. This is never an easy road — they have to want it with all their hearts, sometimes working at a job that is menial in comparison to the money they once made. But many will tell you that with it comes a peace that surpasses their understanding. They develop a "can do" attitude when someone is in their corner working on their behalf.

Now let me further explain the complexities. To say that someone can just leave or get over the stigma, shame or trauma that come as a result of being trafficked is pure ignorance. Many victims suffer a lifetime dealing with the results of being trafficked, taking medication and/or a lifetime of counseling. You can't undo what has been done. You can cope, but the trauma has been imbedded in your brain forever.

However, if one is able to get beyond the trauma and break the chains that bind them, they can be the mouthpiece and inspiration for others to follow. But few make that decision to move to being an advocate, not a victim. You see for so long, they did not have a choice, but were told what to wear, what to do and how to do it; they were unable to think and process for themselves. Life for the victim, after being rescued, is sometimes so uncertain that they would rather stay in what is familiar than move into a future of uncertainty. Those who choose the road to life are incredibly gifted to help others who are in the same situation. We also must remember, that it is difficult for any human who has not traveled this road before to understand the mentality of those trapped in the web of human sex trafficking.

I would like to share a story about one of our successes, with names changed to protect the victim and location.

The first contact I had with Mary was during a festival season. She had been dancing for a very long time and kept the roses and contact cards that we give to the dancers at each visit. The club where she and her boyfriend worked performed live sex acts and was touted as one of the raunchiest clubs in our area. Mary had held onto the contact card for over two years, wanting to call but never summoning the courage to do so. When she finally called, she sounded desperate; she said she would do anything, including cleaning toilets. Something about her made me believe in her, so we proceeded to take the entire family under our wing. We helped with clothing, food, personal items, jobs and money to pay utility bills. We took them to church and even gave them our personal cell phone. Many, many of our team members shared in helping the family get on their feet. Mary and her boyfriend were with us about a year when suddenly Mary's brother took his life. This devastation did not happen at an opportune time in the journey with this family. Nonetheless Mary, her boyfriend and kids decided to move to Ohio to see if they could get a fresh start.

That started their journey. After a very long year of moving in and out of jobs, both Mary and her boyfriend landed very good jobs and began to flourish. Subsequently, I received a telephone call from her, and the conversation that followed was nothing short of a miracle.

Not only was she doing well, but the entire family had moved into wholeness. She married the man she was with, and the children were doing well. Both Mary and her husband made the decision to move beyond their victimization. This was a dream come true and a real testimony as to what one can do, if given the love, support and proper tools to move into that new realm. Not only had they moved into wholeness, but they have also offered support to those caught in that same web of brokenness. Their life now consists of giving back to others.

What can or should be done about this issue of human sex trafficking? In my opinion, there should be more victim advocates, more awareness campaigns and more teams willing to go to the dark underworld of sex to bring a message of hope and love to those who are entrapped. This may be the only genuine expression of love that the victims get to experience. Yes, it is costly and it rips at the very core of womanhood, but I believe that is what we are called to do: love one another, for it is that love that can break any barrier.

Iona Rudisill
Program Operations Manager
Baltimore Child Abuse Center

Iona Rudisill

On a Friday afternoon in 1995, I was wrapping up at work as a Child Protective Services social worker in the District of Columbia, Maryland and Virginia area, when I received a report regarding a young child alleged to have been sexually abused. Police investigators found her in poor physical condition. At only 2 years old, the child was already obese and appeared to have multiple sexually transmitted infections. During the course of this investigation, we discovered this innocent 2-year-old child was being sold for heroin by her mother, was diagnosed with five sexually transmitted diseases and was carrying over 30 extra pounds on her small frame. While there were no anti-trafficking laws enacted at this time to fully address the enslavement this child was experiencing, her mother was convicted of several child abuse infractions, including the production of child sexual abuse images, also known as child pornography.

This was my first encounter with human trafficking as a professional, and the realization that people were still being sold in our society shook me to the core. Through the years since, I have been employed at two accredited Children's

Advocacy Centers in Maryland. At both of those centers, I worked on cases that clearly dealt with trafficking, but some of these cases couldn't be prosecuted as such because the legislation didn't yet exist.

Forms of enslavement and bondage have existed since the creation of time, and through the years it has extended through different definitions. The Egyptians attempted to strip the dignity from a large populous of Jewish culture through enslavement and bondage. The Roman Empire attempted to rob young boys of their innocence by forcing them to be sold as love toys, known as catamites, to priests and others. The Europeans stole millions of African men, women, boys and girls from their native lands to produce commercial gain, without any regard to the value of human life.

Although, the president of the United States signed the Emancipation Proclamation in 1863 to stop the horror of the practice of colonial slavery in this country, slavery still didn't stop. It never has. In 2000, our federal government finally recognized legislation was needed to stop the continued enslavement of people in our country, and acted with the creation of the Trafficking of Victims Protection Act. Even so, human trafficking is a lucrative, multi-billion dollar industry supported by an underworld of organized crime, and it continues to exist today.

In February 1985, Robert E. "Bud" Cramer, a District Attorney in Madison County, Alabama, founded the National Children's Advocacy Center and introduced the Children's Advocacy Center model to the world. Cramer later became a U.S. Congressman and continued to champion for better child protection laws and the Children's Advocacy Center approach. In doing so, he helped create a better qualitative response and systems approach to child abuse.

For years prior, when a suspicion of abuse was reported, a child would have to endure multiple interviews in different locations by several different professionals. There are now more than 800 Children's Advocacy Centers nationwide, providing services to hundreds of thousands of children and youth on a daily basis who have experienced various forms of trauma. The Baltimore Child Abuse Center was the first Children's Advocacy Center established in Maryland and only the third in the country. Since 2007, the Center has been an active member of the Maryland Human Trafficking Task Force, recognizing the importance of developing and implementing a comprehensive response to the sexual trafficking of minors. Over the past 23 years, I have encountered thousands of youth who have experienced sexual trauma and witnessed violent crimes. Survivors of sexual trafficking often have a history of abuse, as do chronic runaways, which makes them highly vulnerable to being trafficked.

Children's Advocacy Centers must have a comprehensive response to human trafficking. I worked as a forensic interviewer for over 16 years, and was trained in several nationally recognized forensic interview protocols. In 2011, I developed a forensic interview script for use with domestic minor sexual trafficking victims. Since that time, it has been used at Baltimore Child Abuse Center in over 40 interviews. Along with colleagues from the Maryland Human

Trafficking Task Force, I contributed to the development of a forensic interview guideline now used throughout the country for cases involving domestic minor sexual trafficking. In recognizing that a comprehensive response needs to include prevention and community outreach, Baltimore Child Abuse Center began offering trainings and family advocacy services were expanded to address the unique needs of trafficking survivors.

Baltimore Child Abuse Center is an independent, nonprofit organization with a history of success in the field of child protection through its collaborative approach and partnerships with a variety of public and private agencies. These agencies include: the State's Attorney Office, Department of Social Services, local, state and federal law enforcement agencies, the University of Maryland, Mercy Hospital and the Department of Health and Mental Hygiene. Partnerships are vital from an operational systems approach. Nonprofit agencies need to be able to pull from a pool of resources to establish programs and more partnerships need to be established to support the anti-trafficking movement.

As a nationally accredited Children's Advocacy Center, Baltimore Child Abuse Center adheres to the National Children's Alliance's strict set of Standards for Accreditation. These standards require Children's Advocacy Centers to have the organizational capacity and expertise to provide a comprehensive approach to human trafficking. For example, one of the standards requires the development and implementation of a multidisciplinary team with representatives from law enforcement, prosecution, victims' services, and mental health and medical providers – the same structure needed for trafficking cases.

Since the sexual trafficking of minors encompasses many dynamics, survivors cannot be adequately serviced by one or two departments because they often have some combination of medical, psychological, emotional, safety, housing, legal and other needs. Another important standard Baltimore Child Abuse Center ascribes to is cultural competency and diversity. Domestic minor sexual trafficking has no barriers or boundaries; it extends beyond gender, socioeconomic status, race, culture and sexual orientation. Youth who have been sexually trafficked have been a part of a business structure where they were given a specific language of communication, had a set of rules with detrimental and often lethal consequences, and lived in restricted areas. Therefore, not only are there cultural differences within the population of those being victimized, but domestic minor sexual trafficking is a subculture itself.

Since the majority of youth seen at BCAC have not been trafficked, but are vulnerable to being trafficked, another important standard and part of the continuum of care is victim support and advocacy. When Baltimore Child Abuse Center serves a youth with a history of running away to areas where commercial sex exploitation is prevalent, and they have a history of abuse, specific preventative measures and services are provided.

In 2016, Baltimore Child Abuse Center served 1,152 children and adolescents with forensic interviews, medical services and victim support and advocacy. Over 780 professionals were trained on human trafficking in six different states, and 89 partner organizations helped raise financial support and awareness for the necessary services that the Center provides to youth and families who have experienced various traumas. The Mandated Reporting Website, created and maintained by the Center, provided understanding to the importance of reporting suspected cases of domestic minor sexual trafficking because it is child sexual abuse. Baltimore Child Abuse Center also began a partnership with the University of Maryland to work on expanding the response of labor and sexual trafficking of minors, throughout the state of Maryland.

While significant strides have been made, Baltimore Child Abuse Center continues to grow its anti-human trafficking program to raise awareness and reduce the vulnerability children with a history of abuse have for falling victim to human trafficking. Youth are our future, and the key to the vitality of our society. They need to be valued, respected and recognized as important, not treated as commodities and objects for the pleasure of others. Not to mention domestic minor sexual trafficking can happen easier than people realize. It is for them that I will continue to be a part of the anti-trafficking movement and proponent of the systems approach that seeks not just to decrease the presence of child abuse, but to end it.

Jacquelin Hahn
Senior Case Manager and Housing Director
FAIR Girls

Jacquelin Hahn

There I was, sitting in a crowded courtroom waiting for her fate to be decided. I watched as my young client nervously approached the bench with her attorney. "I see you have decided to accept the plea deal and go with one year in prison for prostitution," said the judge. "Yes, your Honor," her attorney replied as my client burst into tears.

I was stunned by the outcome, as my rehabilitative efforts had helped my client gain employment and housing. She was well on her way to becoming a reliable caregiver for her two children. The shortsightedness of her courtroom sentence made it clear to me that our criminal justice system can grossly fail victims of sex trafficking instead of embracing them as survivors.

It was in that moment that my passion for challenging this injustice took its full form. From that point on, I made the conscious decision to focus my career on fighting to ensure sex trafficking survivors, like this client, receive the help they deserve.

I first learned about sex trafficking in the United States while watching a documentary about the issue in college. I was not only stunned to learn that the issue exists in the U.S., but more shockingly that there aren't a lot of efforts to end it. I have fortunately had the privilege of helping to combat this issue by serving as a senior case manager and housing director, for the last year, at a Washington, D.C., nonprofit that provides direct services for young female survivors of sex trafficking.

When I talk about the work I do, many people are surprised to learn that 90 percent of the 100 clients I have served are U.S. citizens. It is often assumed that survivors of sex trafficking are foreign, while in fact, many of them are vulnerable and impoverished young American girls who fall prey to perpetrators. Every year, approximately 300,000 Americans under 18 are lured into the commercial sex trade. The severity of sex trafficking's prevalence in the U.S. is compounded by a lack of sex trafficking awareness, poverty and women's unequal societal status.

In trying to do my part to combat this societal issue, I have advocated tirelessly for survivors in court and I have witnessed firsthand the scrutinizing judgment they are subjected to by individuals in positions of power. Despite the fact that many of these young women are often victims of modern day slavery, abuse and poverty, our legal system regularly fails these survivors by promoting incarceration as a response to prostitution.

Even though sex trafficking is a major epidemic in the United States, it does not receive enough attention from the public and criminal justice system. As a result, people misunderstand and are sometimes even unaware of the intricacies of sex trafficking. The solution to combating sex trafficking starts with raising awareness and educating the community.

Locally in D.C., there are efforts to raise awareness in schools, law enforcement and the general community, but it is not enough. To continue these efforts, there needs to be more assistance to fund organizations to educate the community on a grand scale. There is very little government funding to help fund nonprofits aimed to help survivors, as well as funds for survivors to rebuild their lives. Many of those who survive sex trafficking are left with lasting mental trauma and a lack of materials, often just the clothes on their back. We need more funding for survivors to be able to get the mental health care they deserve and material basic needs — like clothes, food, shelter and identification — that are essential in order for survivors to heal and rebuild themselves to become functioning, contributing members of society. With combined efforts from the community and government, along with compassion, I truly believe we can greatly minimize the tragedy of sex trafficking on a nationwide level.

Karen A. Kutzner
Program Director, The Well
A program of Worthwhile Wear

Karen A. Kutzner

"Everyone counts, every person on earth
For their whole life, from the moment of birth."

These are lines from a poem I wrote in elementary school – words that still influence my worldview today. I first heard about human trafficking several years ago in my church when it was the focus of a planned justice initiative. Immediately, I knew that I would play a part in this somehow. Not long after, I learned that a young couple from our congregation had started a nonprofit to address human trafficking domestically, in the suburbs of Philadelphia. We met and I agreed to be part of the team to start a residential program for survivors in our area. Through extensive training and interaction with law enforcement and service professionals, I learned that sex trafficking is happening all over our country in plain sight – in cities, suburbs and rural areas. This is a profound human rights issue in the United States today that deserves our attention and concern in the areas of prevention, prosecution and protection. The girls and women subjected to this dehumanizing treatment are deeply wounded on every level – physically, mentally, emotionally and spiritually. I always think that I've heard the worst story until I hear the next story. The extent and impact of sex trafficking is deeper and darker than I ever imagined.

But there is hope, with increased awareness and a willingness to recognize the need for multidisciplinary restorative care. The Well provides long-term housing, counseling, life skills training and transportation; we collaborate with area service providers for recovery services, mental health support, medical and dental care, and educational and vocational coaching. We've been privileged to see healing and change, but there is much more to be done to provide a meaningful chance for a new start.

The women who come to us are survivors. They are resilient, and they are brave. We are committed to see each woman who comes through the door of our home not as a helpless victim, but as a worthy human being with a heart, a history, a soul and a future of freedom.

Kay Chernush
Photographer, President and Artistic Director
ArtWorks for Freedom

Kay Chernush

As an award-winning photographer and the founder and artistic director of ArtWorks for Freedom, I have been documenting modern day slavery around the world since 2005 when I first became aware of the issue. Until then, I had a successful career as an editorial and corporate photographer, traveling the world for major magazines, Fortune 500 corporations, foundations and governmental agencies. Then I undertook an assignment to photograph human trafficking for the U.S. Department of State – and I discovered that slavery still exists, 150 years after we thought it had been abolished. Today it takes different forms, but it exists in every country, hidden in plain sight.

The more I learned during and after that first assignment, the more constrained I felt by traditional documentary photography. I realized that it could not accurately convey the harrowing experience of being enslaved. It left little room for the nuances and complexities of the survivors' stories and their journeys towards healing and reintegration into their societies. Traditional portraiture raises ethical issues by revealing survivors' identities and holding them captive to their past, potentially re-exploiting and endangering them yet again. It also feeds into society's voyeurism and judgment, particularly where prostitution and sex are involved. The aesthetic dilemmas are even more challenging: how to make visually compelling images of something you can't really show.

To expose the evils of modern slavery, I developed an innovative visual approach that uses the survivors' own stories as a starting point for reframing how this issue is portrayed and how it is perceived by the public. I work one-on-one with trafficking survivors, establishing a relationship of trust, photographing them (for themselves only) and listening to their stories. The constructed, layered images that result, inspired by these stories, are intentionally ambiguous, non-representational, even beautiful.

Individual identity — the faces of the survivors — is stripped away and I use accompanying survivor narratives to set up a tension with the images' surface beauty, exposing the underlying horror of what is being depicted. The images thus point the way to universal themes of betrayal, deception, violence, fear, escape, powerlessness, resilience, courage and hope– common reference points from which viewers can draw their own meaning and emotional connection. The resulting series, "Bought & Sold: Voices of Human Trafficking," was first exhibited in large-scale outdoor art installations in cities throughout the Netherlands and was seen by an estimated 300,000 people.

This is when I began to conceive of ArtWorks for Freedom, a 501c3 nonprofit organization which I founded in

2011. Based in Washington, D.C., ArtWorks for Freedom uses the power of art to raise awareness about human trafficking. Working locally and globally and engaging art in all its forms, we are transforming public perceptions, educating individuals, communities and policy makers and inspiring action to put an end to modern day slavery.

We do this through innovative awareness campaigns featuring exhibits, dance, theater, films, multi-media and community conversations that unite artists with grassroots activists, service providers and other key stakeholders.

So far, we have organized large-scale awareness campaigns, museum exhibits and gallery shows in Singapore, Cambodia, Germany, India and in cities around the United States to expose the realities of human trafficking. Over 750,000 people globally have seen and been affected by our work. Partnering with key stakeholders, service providers, survivor organizations and local foundations, we are building an international coalition of artist-activists, whose creativity and imagination can address the nuances and complexity of this dark societal issue.

Our goal for these campaigns is to start many conversations about the issue and to build communities of awareness that work together to effectively eradicate modern day slavery. Collaboration is needed to point to effective solutions.

We act globally and locally, believing in the power of each individual to make a difference. Through the power of art, we seek to amplify the voices of survivors and inspire people from all walks of life to use their unique gifts in the fight against modern day slavery.

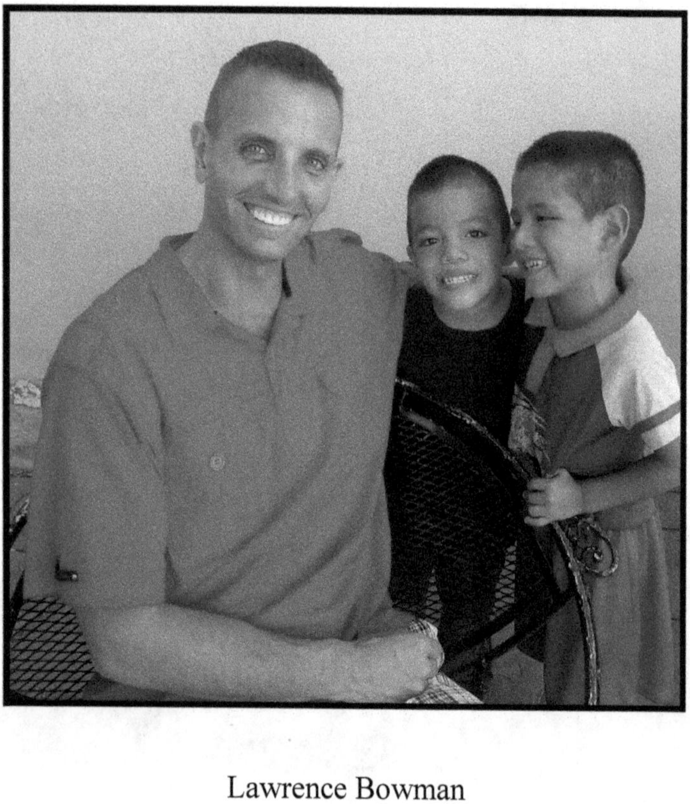

Lawrence Bowman
Founder and Overseer
Orphan Frontier
and
The Heritage Boys Home

Lawrence Bowman

Our focus at Orphan Frontier is to compassionately serve the spiritual and physical needs of abused and abandoned children in the United States and around the world. We diligently labor to serve children by establishing and supporting Christian orphanages, children's homes and ministries for youth who have been rescued from various challenges and troubles. We believe that our work to sustain these ministries with loving and caring staff is a powerful way to give rescued children an opportunity to heal and learn about God's plan for their lives. Within our communities, churches and businesses here in America, our goal is to promote public awareness of various atrocities, such as sexual exploitation, that are being inflicted upon hapless children. We are honored that God gives us the privilege to advocate and be a voice for these youth and their caretakers.

Looking back on my personal life, I believe that the seeds for my life's purpose were sown as a young child. When I was a boy, a very close friend of mine and another acquaintance were both repeatedly sexually abused by their relatives. Thankfully one friend's sexual abuse became known in his childhood, and he found liberty from the oppression. However, for my closest friend, his horrifying experiences as a child were not revealed until he was an adult. Years later his family was shocked to learn some of his gruesome tales. Many have asked how this could have happened. This boy grew up in a wholesome, loving atmosphere. His parents were happily married, and believed that they had set up appropriate boundaries to keep such horrors from happening. He made good grades in school, was social, and seemed to be a happy child with no signs or mention of sexual abuse.

His parents had to learn how not to overwhelm their minds with guilt but instead learn forgiveness for what was not their fault. They did everything they knew to try to protect their children. Unfortunately as in many other cases, sexual abusers seem to have an edge over families' vigilance to keep their children safe.

If I were to talk to people on the streets of America and ask them to define sexual abuse, many would respond with comments along the lines of "being forced to engage in some type of unwanted sex act, or rape." However, sexual abuse occurs in many other forms. Appallingly, an unprecedented number of children and young adults in the United States and worldwide are victims. Many, if not most, of these victims have no voice to cry for help.

As I travel the world to serve abused and abandoned children living in orphanages, I get to sit down with them and listen to some of their stories. Their testimonies of what they lived and persevered through before they were set free are hard to imagine. In listening to their personal accounts, I am quite often reminded that a terrifying reality does exist and is ongoing for many individuals. At any given moment young girls and boys and young adults are being violated, raped and sexually exploited — all for the quick thrill of predators' twisted fantasies.

Far too often I read magazine articles and watch news reports of people being sold into prostitution around the world. In the past, I remember reading and hearing some of these stories, and cringing with great sadness for people I have never known. I would pause to pray to God to deliver and heal them; however, I never felt peace after my prayers. I always felt as if I was somehow supposed to be involved, but the meaning then was unclear to me.

Then a little over two years ago the Lord convicted my heart that the answer to my prayers was *me*. I thought about this, and recalled countless testimonies in the Bible where God used people to accomplish His will. My heart was moved with compassion and a rich understanding for what I must do. I felt God compel me with courage that I should go! I needed to see with my own eyes these precious people—victims living inside brothels where they are forced to be sex slaves.

During one of my trips to southeast Asia, I got into a mototaxi and rode into one of many dark red light districts. As soon as I crossed into this section of the city, I could not believe my eyes. It was worse than I had seen in news reports. Street after street was filled with adolescent girls standing in front of bars and shops. They were provocatively dressed in clothing supplied by their pimps. Many of these young ladies were talking to one another as if they were simply hanging out at a local shopping mall for entertainment; but whenever a man would walk by, one or two girls would strike up a conversation with him.

There were sights that made my stomach turn and my emotions run high in anger. I saw many American and European men walking down these streets. Out of all the men in the world, these ones should certainly not be there! They casually strolled by as if they were in some amusement park, seeming not to not care that the brothel they freely roamed was filled with sex slaves who could not freely leave. Their eyes happily checked out every girl they passed; some seemed to be indecisive about who they would choose to buy for sex. To them, each girl was nothing but a piece of meat.

I then began to wonder about these men's families back home in their own countries. Surely most of them had wives and children of their own. What would they think if they saw their wife or one of their children standing on the streets with no way to escape? I came to the conclusion that they probably did not consider such thoughts. Their conscience has been so seared with a hot iron that they feel no shame in their perversion. My heart overwhelmingly began to cry for their families—clueless that their loved one has perpetrated abominable acts against girls and boys.

Such stories from Asia are hard to read and think about, but this is the reality there for many children and young adults. However, sexual exploitation is not limited to southeast Asia. It occurs all around the globe. I personally have seen girls and boys, women and some men in bondage to sexual abuse. It happens in Asia, Africa, Europe, and all over the Americas.

I recall once being in Tijuana, Mexico, where many Americans cross the United States-Mexico border to have cheap sex. There I saw hundreds of women standing on the streets being guarded by gang members. I was astonished to see a teenage girl being prostituted on the street; even more troubling was that she was guarded by a paid police officer to ensure against her escape. (I secretly video-taped this and it is available to see on my Facebook page.)

These are appalling reports, I understand. It is difficult for me to share these stories. And yet I have seen the horrors with my own eyes, and I am responsible to speak up on behalf of these victims and sound the alarm.

Still, there is a greater shock for many than what I have already written. The dark and appalling secret of sexual exploitation in America is slowly coming to light. It is something that few want to talk about or consider. Many say that this problem does not exist in America because we see little of it on the open streets and public squares. Most Americans do not want to know or accept that sex slavery, exploitation and paid rape are occurring in their local neighborhoods. But it is happening—right over there in that private home, business or hotel.

The sexual exploitation of children and young adults is growing into an overwhelming epidemic in our nation. It is now proliferating throughout all segments of society, and sadly even reaching into some of America's churches. We live in perilous times, and the proof of this is that predators are preying upon the innocent inside our safe havens.

God warns in Hosea 4:6 saying, "*My people are destroyed for lack of knowledge...*" God has warned us that ignorance is not an excuse. Therefore, as much as it grieves my heart to share these stories, I choose to stand in the gap and sound the alarm. As individuals, families and churches begin to comprehend what is happening in their own backyards, they are faced with only two choices: reject the truth and do nothing, or arise and do something about it.

A greater understanding of these terrible crimes will make it more difficult for predators to prey on the innocent. Another reason for the rise in sexual abuse against children and young adults in churches is due to our tendency to be too trusting of others. Churches are to be a place of trust, where we can be free from worry and find care and love with other people. Trust helps us to be able to establish healthy strong relationships with other individuals and families. At the same time, this good thing makes people—particularly within religious communities—easy targets. Predators know that most people in the church let down their guards with others in the church. They take advantage of that trust to secretly abuse and hurt others. We must be wise and not ignorant of these vices.

As stated previously, sexual exploitation is happening everywhere in all segments of society. Within the last year, almost every day American news agencies have had some type of report about someone being arrested for sex crimes. For example, in Georgia, an EMT and a fireman were both arrested in a sting operation for trying to have sex with a child. A Los Angeles Sheriff's psychologist was arrested on account of child sex crimes. A nonprofit official who labored to help troubled children was arrested for committing sex crimes against a child. A famous former Indy race car driver was sentenced for 25 years for sexually abusing a child. A police detective whose job was to investigate online crimes against children had inappropriate contact with two young teens. Even our military has had problems. The Pentagon released a report about uncounted numbers of military cases of sexual exploitation. Military personnel have been arrested in the civilian world for inappropriate relationships with children. And we have all heard about Jared Fogle, who worked for Subway and was sentenced to prison for buying sex with children and other sex crimes.

Again, these are just some of countless stories that have recently happened right here in America. I could list page after page of stories of other police officers, Catholic priests, Disney and Seaworld employees, sports stars, teachers, and many other recognizable people, all going to jail for taking advantage of and sexually abusing children and young adults.

We Americans must be enlightened that sexual exploitation is happening all around us. Just in case you may not be totally convinced yet that this exploitation of children and young adults is out of control in America, consider what the statistics plainly report. First, contrary to popular belief, poverty is not the main cause of sexual exploitation. The FBI, the Department of Justice and local police departments in every state all report that the buying and selling of people and children for sex now occurs in every demographic, social and economic segment of our society. Both the 2.5 million children who experience homelessness each year as well as the suburban rich and middle class children are being preyed upon for illicit sex. Not just the poor children of America, but all children and young adults are at risk; even the children within your community are in danger.

The U.S. Department of Justice reports that approximately 300,000 children are sexually exploited, and thousands of adults are trafficked each year in the United States. The FBI reports that the average age of children who are forced into prostitution is 11 to 13. These vile troubles plague every state, city and town. Just pick up the newspapers and read the headlines. It won't take long to find a new arrest for the buying and selling of persons in your community.

Sex trafficking is a big money business. It generates billions of dollars annually. Many factors contribute to the proliferation of sexual exploitation. The first major factor is ignorance and/or disbelief of what is happening within our own backyards. The second is lack of empathy and desire to get involved to help others in need. Another factor is social problems. In our great country, on average 149,000 children are physically abused each year; 899,000 children (12 out of every 1,000) are confirmed to be victims of abuse or neglect; 450,000 children are in the foster care system. The U.S. Border Patrol estimates that on average 100,000 unaccompanied children cross the U.S. border annually. And more and more children are growing up in divorced homes, and even worse, fatherless homes.

It can be easy to nod at these statistics, but unwisely disregard the potential threat in your own community. Detaching our minds from thinking about these issues does not stop sexual predators from searching out their next victim, even within your family. Sexual abusers prey upon families' passive thinking. They watch us and our families; they learn our weaknesses and vulnerabilities, and at the precise apathetic moment they strike.

Just because we do not see prostitutes standing on street corners does not mean that business is declining. On the contrary, it is increasing. In this modern age of technology, sexual predators no longer need to roam the street corners to find illicit sex. Now they can use the internet to find their victims. At any given moment they can click onto Craigslist or Backpage and find people being sold for sex in every city across America. Smart phones have increased accessibility as well. Young people and adults increasingly are becoming more comfortable with talking to strangers on social apps. These apps can give clever predators greater opportunities to win over the trust of naive individuals into fake relationships. They start up seemingly innocent chats with children and young adults and entangle their prey with flattery. Slowly but surely they build trust with the victim, until one day even your own loved one has been mentally groomed to trust the predator. Then, before he or she can escape, they have been kidnapped, raped, abused, or forced into sex slavery in one of many fashions.

This is the reality in our communities every day. As you are reading this book, someone in your vicinity is being preyed upon without even knowing it. Someone is being coerced and groomed by a sexual predator.

One of the saddest pieces of information I have heard from civil servants is that our law enforcement and social servants are too overwhelmed to successfully mitigate these troubles anymore. In fact, they are begging for help. I have spoken to many, and all say that they welcome more individuals, churches and organizations to join in the battle and assist. They are on the front lines, and they understand that they cannot arrest us out of these problems. They need help from concerned and caring individuals within our communities who will arise to this hour's occasion. This is a major reason that many cities are starting community coalitions in which law enforcement, private organizations, and churches all work together. We need each other to fight this battle.

Law enforcement officers and many private organizations are soliciting for people to get involved. Whenever I talk to churches, organizations, and businesses, I plead with the hearts of their people to see that our neighbors and our world need us. The government can only make law to deter lawlessness. The police can only arrest people after a crime is committed. But you and I can get involved to help.

We should continue to educate ourselves on what is happening near and far from us so that we can be wise servants with good understanding among our neighbors. And we should arise out of our comfort zones, and get involved in the lives of people. Invest yourself in the life of another person. Not every one of us is called to oversee an organization. Not every one of us is meant to be in the public forum; but all of us are called to open our lives and to love and care for another person.

We ought to wake up with an awareness that life is not about ourselves, but it is about others. When we have this mentality within ourselves, we then can be motivated to go out to serve others among the daily responsibilities of life. Then we shall see the world be moved toward a better place.

Now, what will you do?

Michele Clark
Executive Director
ArtWorks for Freedom

Michele Clark

I have been involved in the anti-trafficking world for over 15 years, involving both policy and program experience combating human trafficking on five continents. I am currently the executive director of ArtWorks for Freedom, a nonprofit organization offering a radical new approach to raising awareness about human trafficking by using the transformative power of the arts and the strength of local communities. I am also an adjunct professor at the Elliott School of International Affairs of the George Washington University in Washington, D.C., where I teach courses on human trafficking, women's rights and modern dissident movements. I was also the director of the Anti-Trafficking Unit at the Organization for Security and Cooperation in Europe, based in Vienna, Austria. The mandate of our office was to assist 56 member states to implement their anti-trafficking commitments. I also worked as the co-director of the Protection Project at the Johns Hopkins University School of International Studies, a human rights research institute focused on ending human trafficking.

In 1998, I was living in Israel and teaching at the

University of Haifa. It was an historic era; in 1989, Mikhail Gorbachev allowed the Soviet Jews, who had been protesting for the right to leave, to exit the Soviet Union and join their families in Israel. In less than 10 years, over one million Jews entered Israel to make a new life as free citizens, increasing the population of their new country by 20 percent. In addition to my work at the university, I also volunteered at a humanitarian center that worked alongside the government to offer assistance to these new immigrants in their early days in the country.

One Saturday afternoon, some of my friends went to a picnic on the beach. I went along expecting to spend a pleasant afternoon in the sun, and had no idea that this day would change my life forever. At one point I looked up to recognize my friend Rita getting out of her car. I walked over to greet her and noticed a young woman getting out of the passenger side. Unlike the rest of us, dressed in shorts and T-shirts, she wore a minidress and high heels, and looked as if she were going to a cocktail party instead of a picnic at the beach. She was tall and blonde and moved with deliberate grace across the sand. Inexplicably I felt drawn to her, and I asked Rita who she was. Her name was Olga; Rita had met her in the port area of Haifa because she seemed very unhappy. Rita brought her to the picnic because she thought one of us could help her. I started to talk to her in a mixture of Russian and Hebrew and, drawing heavily on one cigarette after another, she answered my questions. Her story is one that I now know to be so typical of that time. She was from Ukraine. Her husband, an alcoholic, left her with two children. They lived with her elderly parents who depended on her for their income since they were no longer receiving their government pensions. Unable to find work that could provide for everyone, she accepted a job offer from a stranger to work as a hostess in a tourist hotel in Eilat, Israel's resort area. Instead, she was forced to prostitute herself in Haifa's port district.

After she told me her story, she looked straight at me, into my soul. I looked at her and we both knew, in that moment, that there was nothing I could do for her. In that moment of painful recognition, the world seemed suddenly so very broken. Why was this normal? Hundreds of people walked past her every day and no wanted to know, what was wrong with this picture? A young mother, a brave daughter, should not have to be selling sex in the port district of Haifa. I had never felt so helpless as I did when she turned to leave with Rita. That night and for weeks after, I felt Olga's presence hovering over me as I taught my classes, walked along the Haifa beaches, or went grocery shopping on my way home from work. Olga came with me even into my dreams. And slowly a resolve began to form. Rita had done something – she had stopped. Perhaps I could find a way to do something as well. I could not help Olga but perhaps there was something I could do so that others like her would not be trapped into a life of brutal abuse and exploitation.

In December 2000, I returned to Washington, D.C. Friends and former colleagues had been part of the broad coalition that led to the passage of the U.S. Trafficking Victims Protection Act that ushered in an unprecedented series of global and domestic actions to prevent trafficking and assist women like Olga. This became my fight also and I knew I had found my place.

I talk to many good-hearted people who hear about human trafficking and respond with great compassion. But after writing a check, they wonder what else they can do. They have their own personal callings and are not going to run off to join an anti-trafficking organization. Does this mean that there is no place for them?

Not at all.

I have met men and women, students and retirees, moms and management consultants who have found ways to combat human trafficking in their own circles of influence in very powerful ways. Here are two examples.

A mother with young children is on the board of a nonprofit that works with trafficked children. She has been able to grant proposals, lead a strategic planning initiative and become involved in different programmatic activities – even including her family where appropriate. She has turned her anti-trafficking commitment into a family affair and is not only providing great services to her organization, but is also raising up children who see that combating human trafficking is a normal and necessary part of life.

A recent college graduate, who had taken my human trafficking class, was at a staff meeting with her new employer (a youth services agency) when she realized that many of the youth participating in her organization's programs were vulnerable to trafficking. Because she knew what she was talking about, her supervisors listened to her and now the agency has formally included anti-trafficking into its mission statement.

I would say that the potential for individuals to do much good where they are is a vast and untapped resource. The FBI says that most of the cases it investigates are brought to their attention through tips from people who recognize that something is wrong and do something about it. This is why I am a great believer in awareness – the right kind of awareness, the kind that engages the heartstrings as well as the brain cells, that creates empathy that leads to active engagement. Ending trafficking in this country has to involve first a change of heart; we have to wake up to the fact that young women are being brutally exploited in our communities, and that this should never be normal. No social transformation movement has ever been successful if it depended exclusively on legislation. We have good legislation in this country. We need a lot more strong and willing hearts.

Susan Esserman
Founder and Director
University of Maryland Support, Advocacy, Freedom, and Empowerment (SAFE) Center for Human Trafficking Survivors

Susan Esserman

While I have spent much of my career in the field of international trade in government and in the private practice of law, over the last few years, my work on behalf of survivors of human trafficking has increasingly captured my interest and touched my heart.

I was first approached to assist in efforts to fight sex trafficking in India, where I had spent considerable time on behalf of the U.S. government as Deputy U.S. Trade Representative (USTR) and more recently, on behalf of clients in the private practice of law. Instead of undertaking this work in India, I decided I needed grounding in our own efforts to combat trafficking in the U.S. I was stunned to learn the disturbing extent of trafficking and tremendous need for assistance here in this country. So I have dedicated my efforts right here at home.

Through the pro bono program of my law firm, Steptoe & Johnson, I began representing women mainly from Mexico and Central America who were forced into the sex trade in the metropolitan Washington, D.C., area. I helped them apply for the "T" visa, a special nonimmigrant visa available to trafficking victims who cooperate with law enforcement investigations into the trafficking. The women's stories were tragic and heartbreaking and sadly similar: Typically, a vulnerable young immigrant woman from a broken home with little or no educational or job opportunities is lured by a trafficker with promises and gifts. Once in the U.S., she learns that the job that awaits is forced prostitution, where she is compelled to have sex as many as 30 times in a single day and often working seven days a week. And then she is forced to hand over money paid to her to the trafficker and his ring. These women live in appalling conditions; the traffickers often brutally beat them and threaten harm to their children and family in their home country if they should try to escape.

Traffickers around the world use the same tactics whether they are trafficking U.S.-born youth or women or girls from other countries. They target people's vulnerabilities, promising love to women and girls who may have been abused or neglected, promising gifts to youth who may have been raised in poverty, stability to those with broken homes, and job opportunities that sound like dreams come true. For my clients born in other countries, those dreams soon turn into nightmares in the U.S.

Several factors impelled me to get more involved with the issue of human trafficking. I had begun to take on a number of clients who had been trafficked in Prince George's County, Maryland. I formed close working relationships with law enforcement investigators working in Prince George's County, and they began referring survivors to me directly.

After representing a number of trafficking victims in their legal cases, I came to see a common pattern among my clients: Even though we were successful in securing legal benefits for them, they were unable in any meaningful way to escape the trauma of their trafficking. Even years after their escape, they are battling memories of trauma and struggling to regain their footing.

To address this issue, I worked with the University of Maryland to establish the University of Maryland Support, Advocacy, Freedom, and Empowerment (SAFE) Center. The SAFE Center opened in May 2016 in a location near the College Park campus. We chose this location in part because of its location in Prince George's County, close to the Langley Park neighborhood where sex trafficking is prevalent. The SAFE Center is a joint effort of the University of Maryland, Baltimore, and the University of Maryland, College Park through the MPower program. We provide comprehensive services to trafficking victims, regardless of nationality, gender or age. That means we provide services to foreign nationals and domestic U.S. victims, women and men, youth and adults, and victims of labor trafficking as well as sex trafficking. We also conduct research and advocacy to address trafficking on a systemic level.

The demand for the SAFE Center's services has exceeded our expectations. Program services include legal advocacy and representation, the provision of immediate, basic needs, mental health counseling services, intensive case management, and basic primary medical care. The SAFE Center is also developing economic empowerment programs to help survivors reintegrate into the community, restore dignity and build a sustainable future for themselves and their families. The Center's research and policy advocacy efforts are designed to identify critical knowledge and practice gaps, to inform the priorities of legislators and to strengthen the provision of services to trafficking survivors.

We don't do this work alone. Since we opened our doors, we have had more than 30 students intern with us, doing critical research, helping us provide services and developing programs and protocols. We are fortunate to be able to draw on the intellectual resources of the University's top departments and programs. The School of Public Policy is the SAFE Center's administrative home at the University of Maryland, College Park; at the University of Maryland, Baltimore the SAFE Center's administrative home is the School of Social Work. The SAFE Center also collaborates with the School of Nursing to provide basic medical services to trafficking survivors, the College of Arts and Sciences to provide interpretation and translation assistance, the College of Behavioral and Social Sciences to provide counseling services through psychology clinics and undergraduate law internships, the School of Law to provide student externships and law clinic expertise, and the School of Business to provide consulting on economic empowerment programming.

More than 50 years ago Dr. Martin Luther King Jr. called on our nation's conscience to make real for all within its borders America's founding ideals: life, liberty, and the pursuit of happiness. But the tens of thousands of human trafficking victims in America know neither liberty, nor happiness; their lives play out against a backdrop of intolerable cruelty with little hope of salvation. So much remains to be done. Only with a sustained and broad-based effort can we truly free the victims of human trafficking from the bondage and the trauma they endure. We at the SAFE Center are grateful to be working with so many partners at the University of Maryland and in the community in this effort.

SECTION IV

THERAPY AND HEALTH CARE

(Ravi pictured on the left)

Dr. Anita Ravi

Physician and Researcher

PurpLE Clinic

Dr. Anita Ravi

In the fall of 2013, I was in the final year of my medical training as a family medicine physician, when my mentor forwarded me an email that said "FYI, thought this might interest you." The email was about Mount Sinai's Adolescent Health Center's "Conference on Child Abuse and Neglect and Sex Trafficking" which was being co-directed by Dr. Angela Diaz, a national leader in child trafficking. As a physician who went into medicine to address the intersection of gender-based violence, health and the legal system, this was an unfamiliar topic to me that sparked immediate interest. Attending Dr. Diaz's conference was a transformative experience; experts from multiple organizations and professional backgrounds discussed the issue of sex trafficking from a health care lens and provided a comprehensive overview of the depth and complexity of the issue in the United States. In looking back, receiving that "FYI" email completely changed the trajectory of my future work.

Inspired by this conference, I conducted a research project to interview incarcerated sex trafficking survivors on

Rikers Island regarding their health experiences while trafficked, as well as for advice they had for the health care system to better serve this population. In the process of designing this study, I met with community-based organizations in New York City and learned that an acute need for trafficking survivors, particularly those who were undocumented or uninsured, was to have access to a trauma and trafficking-sensitive health home.

As a result, in 2015, I partnered with the Institute for Family Health, one of New York State's largest Federally Qualified Health Center networks, to launch the PurpLE (Purpose: Listen and Engage) Clinic in New York City. We spent one year planning the launch of the clinic, with the goal of offering person-centered health care for survivors of sexual violence, including sex trafficking. Key stakeholders, including sex trafficking survivors and community-based organizations serving survivors, shaped the clinic's prominent features, such as implementing a trauma-sensitive intake and triage process, longer visit lengths and multidisciplinary team collaboration.

The PurpLE Clinic runs weekly, and connects patients with The Institute's safety-net services of screening and enrolling eligible patients in health insurance, providing affordable medication access, connecting patients with dental care, mental health services and acupuncture, and initiating care navigation services to address housing, legal, and nutritional needs. We are proud to be able to serve survivors and their families, regardless of age, gender or insurance status.

It has been wonderful to see the engagement of a multi-disciplinary response to trafficking. To have sectors such as medical, legal, public health and social work come together and collaborate towards assisting survivors and solving the broader policy related issues associated with trafficking.

As a health care provider, the one area that I hope will be addressed in the coming years is shifting the culture of medicine toward a person-centered practice. The people we work with who have experienced trafficking value characteristics in physicians that are simple and essential but become novel practice as medical training progresses: empathy, compassion and acceptance. Prioritizing these characteristics when selecting and training physicians, as well as features such as longer visits and affordable health care, are critical for the medical community to strengthen its mission to support trafficking survivors seeking health care.

Irene Jacobs
Therapist, Program Director
Willow House at The Meadows

Irene Jacobs

Early in my career, I found myself working with trafficking victims. I worked as a counselor for Catholic Charities. Catholic Charities had a unique year-long residential program for women who were victims of domestic sex trafficking and human trafficking. The program was called Dignity and included a safe house. Kathleen Mitchell founded the Dignity Program based off her own history with domestic sex trafficking.

I provided trauma-focused therapy for the women at the Dignity safe house. I facilitated a weekly trauma recovery therapy group. I also saw each woman for individual therapy. Their therapy involved an eclectic approach of cognitive behavioral therapy, dialectical behavioral therapy and emotion regulation. Aside from therapy, the Dignity Program provided community connection assistance for wrap-around services such as chemical dependency detox, medical assistance, psychiatry and life skills. Many of the women who completed the program have gone on to lead successful lives.

The women typically entered the Dignity Program with a look of fear and loss in their eyes. There was a dullness and a lack of spark, almost as if they were disconnected from themselves and just a few steps away from death. The women were easily overwhelmed and often struggled to shower and brush their teeth. They required guidance with everything, from making the bed to filling out paperwork.

Almost immediately I began to realize how challenging this population was. I learned that they had significant attachment issues which flared up as borderline personality disorder. Many of them struggled with cravings and urges for substances and sex. They had active and passive histories of self harm, disordered eating, suicidal ideation, panic attacks, spending, childhood sexual/physical/emotional abuse, covert childhood trauma of abandonment and enmeshment and adult sexual trauma.

One of my most difficult cases was a younger woman who came into the program bruised from her pimp's beatings. Her pimp was angry that she did not make her quota. He beat her, doused her with water and forced her to sleep next to the cooler unit in the hotel room. The cold air circulated in her direction as she lay there wet and hurting. After a couple of hours he grabbed her, kicked her, punched her, choked her and threw her through the hotel room window. I remember feeling horrified that a human being could treat another human being in such a deplorable manner. She stayed in the program about a week.

Her few days with us were filled with tears, nausea, vomiting, trembling, panic attacks and a desperate desire to return to her pimp. Her symptoms were not from chemical withdrawals. She was withdrawing from love addiction and a betrayal bond. She returned to her pimp against the advice and warnings from staff. All of the staff knew that her days were counted. I didn't understand why instead of feeling relieved to have escaped her abusive pimp she felt terrified of living life without him.

I began researching why women stay with an abusive person. I found plenty of information around the topic of domestic violence. The information I found specific to domestic sex trafficking was written by pimps teaching men how to create sexual and emotional dependency. I eventually came across three names that forever changed my professional career: The Meadows, Pia Mellody and Patrick Carnes.

Pia Mellody and Patrick Carnes both developed their therapy modalities while working for The Meadows. Pia's work focused on codependency and love addiction love avoidance. Patrick Carnes developed treatment for sex addiction and betrayal bonds, both of which are factors in domestic sex trafficking.

Pia's model on codependence demonstrates how we lose our ability to be relational with ourselves and others because of relational trauma with our caregivers. The trauma of abandonment from caregivers can set up a child to be addicted to love, people and relationships. The abandonment creates a belief system of "I need someone in my life to take care of me. If I don't have someone in my life to take care of me, that is equivalent to relational death." The abandoned child feels worthless in relation to their partner. Young girls are easily prone to attach to nurturance demonstrated from pimps who play the role of an older boyfriend. Pimps target these lonely girls and brainwash them and/or force them into domestic sex trafficking.

The trauma of enmeshment from caregivers creates codependence of avoidance through caretaking. The enmeshment creates a belief system of "It's my duty to take care of others. I gain value and worth from caretaking." Enmeshment squashes a child's natural spontaneity, therefore they seek intensity. Enmeshment and overt or covert sexual abuse can pave the way for seeking intensity through sexual acting out behaviors. Over time, sexual acting out behaviors can progress to sex addiction via domestic sex trafficking.

Patrick Carnes defines sex addiction as a pathological relationship with sexual behavior. Not all domestic sex trafficking victims are addicted to sex. However, it wasn't unusual for some of the Dignity Program women to struggle with masturbation and sexual acting out with each other. The women were taught sexual boundaries, how to manage triggers and how to show true intimacy and vulnerability.

Trauma goes hand in hand with domestic sex trafficking. Victims become bonded to the intensity, shame and abuse. Patrick Carnes does an excellent job defining the various types of trauma bonding in his book *The Betrayal Bond*. A trauma bond can be so extremely powerful that women stay in life-threatening relationships. Pimps teach other pimps how to create a trauma bond with women. When the bond is strong enough, a domestic sex trafficking victim will do anything for their abuser.

After working over five years with Catholic Charities

and the Dignity Program, which has since closed, I left Catholic Charities to work for The Meadows. During my five years at The Meadows I have continued to work with women struggling with sexual compulsivity and victims of domestic sex trafficking. I am currently the program director for Willow House at The Meadows. Willow House is a female-only treatment facility for women with relationship issues, including domestic sex trafficking. I also provide behavioral health consultation services for Unchained Movement, a program creating awareness and safe housing in Tennessee for trafficking victims. I am honored to continue to provide awareness, healing and hope with this population.

Katherine Hargitt
Licensed Clinical Psychologist
Specialization in Recovery & Reintegration of Survivors of Child Sexual Exploitation

Katherine Hargitt

A succession of serendipitous events on life's path led to my specializing in trauma and the recovery and reintegration of children affected by sexual exploitation and trafficking. Although it is my sincere wish that such work not be necessary, I am grateful to have listened to this calling, as it has allowed me to meet many remarkable individuals and witness the progress made over several decades.

The plight of abused and exploited children first came into my awareness when I was 4 years old. I lived in Italy then, and for Christmas I was given a 45 rpm record of "La Piccola Fiammiferaia." I have a somatic memory of listening to Hans Christian Anderson's fairy tale of "The Little Match Girl." It jolted my awareness, and henceforth I was alert to any stories related to abused and neglected children, runaways, foster children, abandoned children, children who were deemed juvenile delinquents or children who were caught in the middle of wars. The reality of children actually being trafficked specifically for sexual purposes was brought to my attention when I entered adolescence.

My best friend and I were planning to spend the

afternoon at the new shopping center in downtown Brussels, Belgium. To our surprise, however, our mothers forbade us from going there that day. We learned that girls our age had recently been kidnapped and sold into the white slave trade. I was well aware of the red-light neighborhoods then. When out-of-town friends came to visit, it was one of the areas they'd want to see, so my parents would inevitably drive them by the many scantily dressed women soliciting passersby from behind their windows. While the adults around me chuckled, I felt a knot in my stomach. Although these women were smiling, I sensed sadness in the eyes of many. However, I did not yet know that the majority of women in prostitution were not there out of pure choice, and that there was a link between trafficking and prostitution. I didn't understand then the severity of what the white slave trade entailed.

A few years later, I was in Nepal, where I got to know many of the children living in street situations. I witnessed firsthand child abuse, and almost lost a friend to trafficking. Fast forward to the mid 1990s, when I was in Kathmandu again, and learned that it had become a common occurrence for tourists to buy street children for sexual purposes. About a year later, a child sex trafficking ring was uncovered in Belgium. I remember being in a grocery store when the country took a moment of silence to honor the victims. An announcement was made on the PA system, and we all paused. Cars and buses pulled over on the side of the road. More than 350,000 people marched in silence as part of the Marche Blanche organized by the victims' parents.

A slew of questions started to occupy my mind. I wondered, 'How do children who are severely abused, exploited and trafficked heal from such abhorrent experiences? What do they need? Is recovery possible?' And thus, after a career as a teacher, and too many encounters with abused and neglected children, I decided to study psychology. I wanted to learn everything I could about trauma, child sexual abuse and human trafficking, to help these children. At that time, the United States had just signed the Trafficking Victims Protection Act (2000), and I attended a presentation about it in San Francisco. This was the first of the many human trafficking related events I would eventually attend, in the United States and abroad.

Doors began to open, and I had the opportunity to conduct an independent field study in Cambodia, India, Nepal, the Philippines and Thailand. I visited organizations and drop-in centers, stayed at different shelters, and met with survivors of sexual exploitation and trafficking, and their service providers. Although a few of the children I met had lost the twinkle of light and hope in their eyes, and some were dying, I was most surprised by the resilience of many others. Through happenstance, I met some of these survivors six years later while in Brazil for the World Congress III Against the Sexual Exploitation of Children and Adolescents. We have stayed in regular contact since. It is encouraging to know that with adequate support, they were able to resume lives that were as normal as possible. Some even got married and have children now. However, it is clear that access to continued support is vital.

SECTION IV: THERAPY AND HEALTH CARE

Upon my return to the San Francisco Bay Area in 2002, I began to look into what was available in the country in terms of recovery and reintegration services for survivors of sexual exploitation and trafficking. After what I had found in Southeast Asia, I was dismayed at the walls of denial, the lack of knowledge on this issue, and the paucity of services for this population in the United States. Nevertheless I also met remarkable pioneers, such as Norma Hotaling, founder of the Sage Project, and Lois Lee, founder of Children of the Night.

Soon thereafter, I became an intern at Marin County Juvenile Hall, and worked with numerous girls charged with loitering for prostitution. I developed protocols for identification and intervention, tried to raise awareness among staff and professionals, and attempted to organize informational meetings in the community. The notion that children involved in prostitution were actually victims of human trafficking was still very new. Most people turned a deaf ear, and several held to the belief that these girls knew what they are getting into. The head of a safe haven for children, a supposed expert on child sexual abuse, firmly believed that these kids don't want help. Marin County wasn't ready yet to acknowledge that human trafficking was happening in their backyard.

Nonetheless, I persisted in my efforts and brought together heads of Sonoma County nonprofit organizations, as well as survivors. Together we started what eventually became the official Sonoma County Human Trafficking Task Force, actively led by the District Attorney's Office. I also joined MISSSEY's board, and worked closely with its founder, Nola Brantley, on developing a training curriculum for the organization's volunteers. Jenny Williamson, founder of Courage Worldwide, consulted with us as she moved forward to open a much needed shelter home for minor females rescued out of sex trafficking. During that time, I was completing my doctoral dissertation entitled, "Development of a Training Model and Curriculum Outline for Counselors/Advocates of Commercially Sexually Exploited Children in the United States." As interest on the issue of human trafficking grew, I was invited to conduct lectures and trainings for professionals, students and laypersons, here and abroad. I also discussed this topic regularly as part of the mandatory trainings to become certified crisis counselors and advocates for victims of domestic violence and sexual assault. There was now no lack of opportunities to present, as human trafficking had finally become the new 'flavor of the month.' It was, and still is, exciting to witness this explosion of interest, and the related efforts to increase victim identification and services.

While I was striving to raise awareness about child sexual exploitation and trafficking and advocating for services, the issue hit very close to home. One evening, 14 years ago now, I learned that a close family member had become the unbeknownst subject of a relative's perverted interest in child sexual abuse images. The whirlwind of events that followed cast a close light into a justice and victim protection system that had not yet caught up with such forms of violence against children. Hence, justice was not adequately served and support services were not available through the victim compensation program. This personal experience showed me some of the diverse effects such crimes can have on a child, as well as on their family, in both the short- and long-term. It also highlighted how the child's extended family and community can play an essential role in the process of recovery. Unfortunately, the manifestations of trauma are poorly understood, which often leads to further victimizing and stigmatizing those who actually need support.

More recently, I have worked with survivors through my private practice as a licensed clinical psychologist. This is facilitated through the victim compensation program that has finally caught up with the different forms of child sexual exploitation and trafficking, and thus enables victims to access a certain amount of mental health support at no charge. I have also conducted another study on the recovery and reintegration needs of this population. In 2015, as the lead researcher and consultant and for ECPAT International's research project on access to justice and right to remedies, I held discussions with 67 survivors and 72 service providers in Nepal, the Philippines and Thailand. I've also had the opportunity to work as a consultant and external reviewer for a study, led by the United Nations Special Rapporteur on the sale of children, child prostitution and child pornography, that was specific to the care, recovery and reintegration of child victims of sale and sexual exploitation. As a founding member of the Sonoma County Human Trafficking Task Force and the co-chair of HEAL Trafficking's Service Provider Committee, I continue to raise this public health issue to the forefront and bring service providers together toward enhancing the support survivors of human trafficking need as part of their healing process.

Momentous strides have been made in the United States since the enactment of the Trafficking Victims Protection Act. The same is true around the world. Many more organizations, whether governmental or non-governmental, are now working hard to address the different forms of child sexual exploitation and trafficking. Professionals across diverse sectors are receiving much needed training, which in turn leads to increased efforts in prevention, victim identification and services, as well as prosecution of offenders. But much work remains ahead in order to eliminate this form of violence. Poverty and the demand side of human trafficking are significant beasts to tackle: one step at a time, all together.

SECTION V

SURVIVORS AND FAMILY MEMBERS

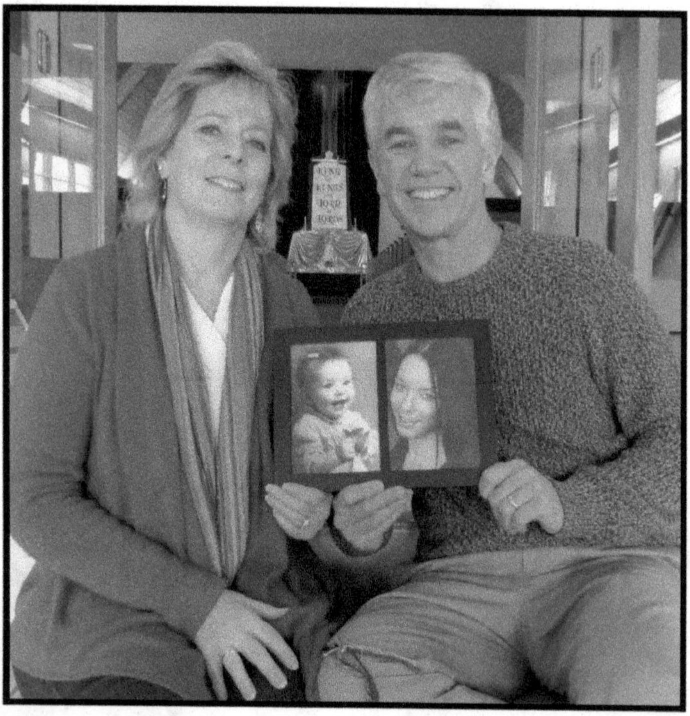

Craig and Lisa McLaughlin

Parents of victim

Hannah's Hope was founded by members of their church.

Craig and Lisa McLaughlin

Hannah was the baby of our family with three older siblings. She was loved and adored by us, and by her friends and church community. When she was a young girl, Hannah, unbeknownst to us, was a victim of repeated sexual trauma. This led to severe anxiety that she continued to deal with for years. As an adolescent, Hannah began dabbling in drugs to deal with her anxiety and the memories of trauma, and at 14 she became addicted to opioid pills. Our daughter had become an addict.

At 16, Hannah returned home after 15 straight months in treatment programs — from an adolescent rehab in Indiana, to a wilderness program in North Carolina, to a therapeutic ranch in Utah. At a recovery meeting once she was back home, she met a 24-year-old man who charmed her into becoming his 'girlfriend.' He was a heroin addict, and he taught her to shoot heroin. To feed his heroin habit, he taught her to shoplift for him. He pawned her guitars and other belongings. He told her to steal family jewelry. He had her panhandling. He took her to The Block in Baltimore and made her work as a dancer and prostitute in one of the strip clubs. This was to feed his habit and hers. He was manipulative and convincing. She was a child.

The struggle of someone in addiction, who wants more than anything to break out, is difficult to watch. Hannah struggled so severely with her addiction, and her attempts at recovery were intense, exhausting, heartbreaking and expensive. Counting up the times Hannah was in detox, rehab, halfway houses and juvenile detention, we realized she was in 22 institutions in five years. Our family never gave up on her, but addiction to heroin was even stronger than the love of family. We tried everything, and she tried everything.

Hannah lost hope of sobriety, and her addiction took her to the streets again and again. Can you imagine the ugly pain when we realized our daughter's picture was on *Backpage.com* under escort services? When we realized our daughter had a "dancer nickname" and a "prostitute nickname?" When we saw bruises on our precious daughter's face inflicted by a john?

In the summer of 2013, Hannah tried again to reach sobriety and chose to go to a halfway house in Florida. Despite what she was told during application, the program had no structure. Hannah was vulnerable to the young men waiting outside the door for any girls who walked out. Her recovery was once again sabotaged. Hannah was on the streets in Florida, and we were in Maryland. For six weeks we received occasional phone calls from her, but she was being controlled by a pimp. Sometimes she would insist she was fine, and other times she told us she was locked in a room and then hang up quickly saying,"They're coming back." Then she wouldn't answer her phone or contact us for days. One day Hannah texted us a photo of herself and two other girls sitting in a private jet, each holding a wad of money. The girls were being trafficked from Florida.

After apparently stopping in Kentucky, they ended up in Ohio where they were locked in a large house. The girls were sometimes allowed to go into the backyard, which was surrounded by a tall, locked privacy fence. Their 61-year-old pimp said that they were a family, and about once a week insisted that they all have dinner together– which was boxed macaroni and cheese. Most times there were no meals, but drugs were available for everyone. Every day men came to the house to be serviced by the girls. And each day the pimp chose which girl was his. Hannah was once taken to witness the pimp and his son severely beat another girl who ran away from the house. At least once Hannah had a gun pointed at her. She was scared but couldn't figure out how to get out, and she had no idea the address of where she was. During these weeks we constantly tried calling Hannah and sent her many text messages telling her to run. We sent her words of love and scriptures for strength. And we sent her the Polaris anti-trafficking hotline number again and again. Periodically we heard back from her.

We had been in touch with Polaris throughout this time, and were cautioned about the violence associated with trafficking and that rescuing needed to be done carefully. Our oldest daughter, Sarah, connected with the Salvation Army in Ohio who works with Polaris, and took guidance from them. After almost a month, Hannah and another girl had the opportunity to run. They called Polaris, who contacted the local Salvation Army, who then sent two women to get the girls, take them to a safe place and arrange to get them into detox. These women were our angels. It is 430 miles from our home in Maryland to Columbus, Ohio. When Hannah was safe and we knew where she was, Craig and our oldest daughter Sarah drove all the way to Columbus, scooped up our daughter, and drove all the way home again in one day.

Hannah struggled so severely with her addiction, but the experiences she had in Florida and Ohio really broke her. She tried recovery again and again, but we could see she had no hope of success. When things were going well she didn't think she deserved it. She knew only one way to feed her drug addiction. She disappeared again and we didn't hear from her for a couple of weeks. One night Craig and I were driving around looking for her at local recovery meetings, and then Hannah called. She was on The Block in Baltimore and wanted to come home. We drove straight there, and were horrified seeing her in the midst of that atmosphere. She was so very traumatized, she was not able to speak a word until we were halfway home, and even then she could only whisper.

Trafficked in Maryland. Trafficked in Florida. Trafficked in Ohio. So broken and traumatized that she could not fully accept that she was worth being properly loved, she could not understand why we still adored her. And without believing she was worth it, she didn't have the strength to keep fighting her addiction. Hannah died of a drug overdose at age 19. But it was the combination of childhood sexual trauma and addiction that left her so very vulnerable to becoming a human trafficking victim.

Trafficking took a tremendous toll on our daughter. But it also took a tremendous toll on all those who loved her: nightmares, sleepless nights, afraid of phone calls, panic at emergency sirens and general fear and distrust of others. One day Lisa saw Hannah being dropped off in front of our house by a pimp, and Lisa reacted by confronting the pimp with screams, shouts and threats, which were all out of character for her. We constantly called and sent texts to one another and our other children to seek or share updates on Hannah. We were consumed with our concerns for her, which made us sometimes forget to give attention to the rest of the family.

In memory of our daughter, our church began an outreach called Hannah's Hope. Hannah's Hope is dedicated to fighting human trafficking both locally and globally. Our mission is to combat this injustice by raising awareness, offering education to at risk populations and bringing hope and restoration to those who have been affected by it.

Shayla Davis

I lost myself to low self-esteem. I always wanted to fit in. I was introduced to selling my body at a young age. I was naïve to the fact that it was human trafficking. They called it "body massages" or something very similar to that. I can't quite think of the word they persuaded me with… So I became accustomed to being called a whore, selling my body and getting high on drugs. That is was what I was told to do. At the time, it felt good. I was high and didn't fully understand what was happening; but when I wasn't high, I would be left so broken and all I wanted to do was die. I had nobody to talk to because I was and still am afraid that I will be judged. In society, it's deemed not normal to have sex for money. I still fear to share my story with loved ones. I have spent seven years feeling lost, selling myself, doing drugs and reaching the point of wanting to commit suicide.

Now I am trying to overcome it all and throw it behind me.

I am also trying to love myself and look at myself in the mirror and say, "*I can do it.*" I really don't even know who I am at times, because my past has me so wounded.

Sometimes I don't see a way out of this... Is it possible to love myself again? Is it possible to be OK with who I am despite the pain I've experienced?

It's easier than we think to get caught up in the definition of sex trafficking; it is dressed up in different ways that don't always look exactly like what is in the movies. In my situation, it was brought to me as "massages," until he asked me to take some pictures naked. I was only 17, a minor, and didn't know what to do. I was manipulated and taken advantage of. They still said it was a massage job, until the doors closed and my phone rung for the first time and it was a call from *Backpage.com*. He did all the talking on the phone and then he glared at me and told me to get ready for a "date." In that moment, I remember being speechless. I asked him to give me a minute. Afraid, I went through the door that was connected to my friend's room and asked her what to do. She responded, "You are only giving massages, don't worry." As I walked back over to the other room, I was told it was game time. The customer, in the other room, asked me how much for a f***. I was confused and didn't know what was going to happen next. That was the moment my life changed forever… It went from me thinking I was getting a job in the massage industry, to being tricked into being pimped. I remember him — my pimp — asking for my money. I questioned it. He replied, "You don't question Daddy! Daddy is going to take care of you." From that day on, I became a victim of human trafficking.

Getting into the game is the easiest, but getting out of it is the hardest.

Being surrounded by so many people giving dirty looks and judgments leaves us scared to speak out and tell someone that we are victims. Instead, we are forced to drown in our pain. We are afraid that if we leave, we won't have anyone to lean on or run to. We are then forced to go back to our pimps, because that's the only love we know. But that isn't really love at all, because they don't care about our wellbeing. If we have more love than judgment, then we can reach out and get the help we need. That is what America needs. I truly believe that all it takes is a genuine heart full of love to save our precious souls. We've been manipulated so long into believing we aren't worth more than selling our bodies for sex. All the beauty is deep inside us survivors, we just struggle to see it.

SECTION VI

ADVOCACY

Aubrey Sneesby
B.A. in Criminology and Criminal Justice
from the University of Maryland
Former co-president of Students Ending Slavery

Aubrey Sneesby

Though sex slavery is the most known type of human trafficking, there are still many myths that are portrayed in our society about it. For example, one of the biggest myths is that there is a certain type of person who 'goes' into sex slavery. This is completely false, and in reality any type of person from any type of background can be susceptible to the sex slavery industry.

Although volunteering and fundraising are extremely important in ending sex slavery, awareness is often understated. Making sure that the real truths of slavery are publicly known can have life-saving results. Everyone has the capacity to raise awareness about the signs and myths of sex slavery, through social media or daily conversations. Every day I hope to help spread the truths of slavery in any way that I can, especially with my peers. Awareness of the facts really is a powerful thing, and that is how Students Ending Slavery hopes to serve the University of Maryland community.

Students Ending Slavery seeks to mobilize students to take part in abolishing modern day slavery in our community, Washington, D.C., and the world by discussing the issues and getting involved any way we can. As I said before, though it seems like a student group is limited in what we can do for victims and survivors of sex slavery, the importance of our awareness campaigns and discussions is very much understated. Making the general population aware of the reality of sex slavery and human trafficking can allow us to expose those myths. When the truths are known by a generation, or those on the University of Maryland campus, we can begin to advocate for change, recognize the signs when we see them in a public area and seek a society where sex slavery is not a daily reality for millions of people. In Students Ending Slavery specifically, we try to do as many awareness and fundraising events as possible. Once there are events that are visible to the University of Maryland population, like our 5K annual fun run in the spring, it stirs up more curiosity around the subject. When these events gain a good amount of attention around our campus and spark the curiosity around the subject of human trafficking, that is when we know we've done a decent job.

I have also worked for the University of Maryland SAFE Center for Human Trafficking Survivors as a research and outreach intern. This newly opened drop-in center for services is an amazing testament to the University of Maryland's commitment to ending slavery, especially around this area. There you can receive case management, legal services, counseling and many more things. Working there, I was able to truly see the problems in our system for trafficking survivors. There are many different pitfalls and obstacles that survivors need to get through daily in order to function and gain actual reconciliation in life. Interning at this center was amazing, and to see how many people are dedicated to eradicating sex slavery and human trafficking in general is inspiring.

Overall, I hope to become one of those people one day. As I go into my last semester of my senior year, I look forward to going out into the world with the knowledge I know and spreading as much awareness and aiding in any way that I can. This issue of sex slavery is a gruesome one that people like to ignore due to its nature. However, while some people choose to ignore, others are suffering. I plan to do my part in ensuring that people stop turning away from others in situations of need. Sex slavery can be eradicated, but we as a society need to have a reality check on how we treat people.

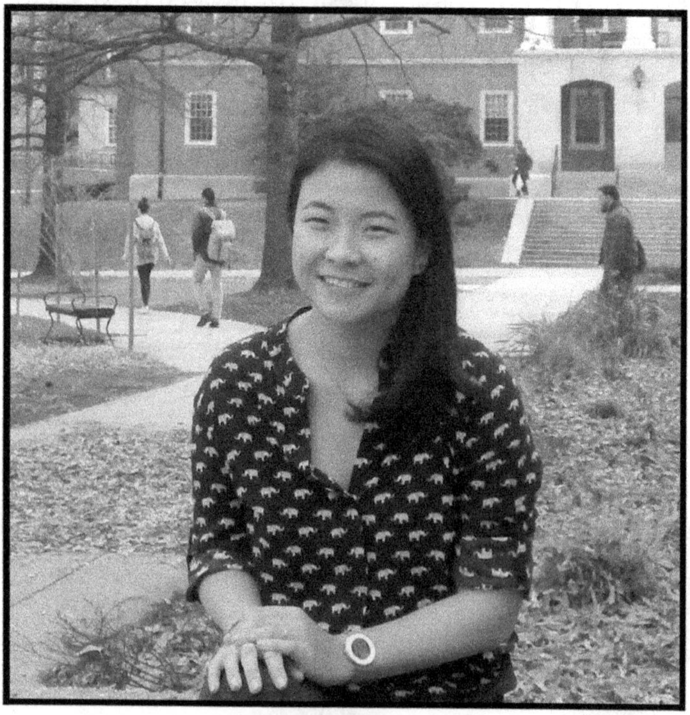

Emily Long

B.A. in Government and Politics

from the University of Maryland

Former co-president of Students Ending Slavery

Social Media Intern at UMD SAFE Center

Emily Long

Last year, I was co-president of Students Ending Slavery at the University of Maryland, and the social media intern at the University of Maryland SAFE Center, a drop-in resource and research center for human trafficking survivors.

In the interest of speaking to solutions, I will recount some of my advocacy and engagement experiences as a college student, as well as a few of the empowerment opportunities I've explored with my peers, namely utilizing social media for social justice. Why is student activism critical to the anti-trafficking movement? Because we are the future. Just as poverty, climate change, and the refugee crisis are massive concerns that will far outlive older generations, human trafficking will not end with our grandparents or parents—or with us, necessarily—but solving these problems can only happen in our lifetimes, not theirs. The recognition of students' and young adults' integral role in abolishing human trafficking is one of the many reasons Students Ending Slavery was created.

The three tiers to Students Ending Slavery's objectives are volunteering, fundraising and raising awareness. Though we do not limit each component as such, they help us address human trafficking around the world, in the DMV area, and at UMD, respectively. Our goals are to ensure that every UMD student knows slavery still exists, to combat trafficking in Maryland and Washington, D.C., and to contribute funds to international organizations that have more experience, reach, and resources than SES does.

My most frequent experience in human trafficking organizations has been with social media and web development; I have been exploring and expanding upon the internet's ability to foster abolitionism. For instance, during my internships with FAIR Girls and the SAFE Center, I established and maintained a social media presence for each organization. This task entailed networking with related organizations and creating original content that followers would share in their own circles. My experience as co-president of SES has been similar, hosting a Facebook page and managing a listserv to keep students engaged. I believe the internet is ideal for raising awareness, but it also has a role to play in terms of taking action.

For every way that the digital world has allowed traffickers to grow their business in buying and selling human beings, there is an opportunity for justice-seekers to combat their growth. For instance, while Backpage allows pimps to advertise women and johns to "order" them for sex with a few clicks, Polaris and many others create the option for internet users to sign a petition or raise awareness in their networks with the same level of ease. I hope to galvanize our tech-savvy generation to use our connectivity powers for good. We have a responsibility to take advantage of the speedy and far-reaching communication that modern technology affords and use it for justice. We ought to stand up, fight and advocate for what so many of us believe in: freedom for all people. We can combine selfie sticks and hashtags to spark and ignite awareness campaigns; we can spend hours shopping online at fair trade websites; we can even tweet to celebrity figures and political leaders alike with our grievances and suggestions for change. For every meme we share or every Instagram filter we use, we should post about the 45 million people who are enslaved and what it will take to serve them effectively.

Sarah Lin
Senior at Rutgers University
Urban Planning and Public Policy Major
International Justice Mission

Sarah Lin

My name is Sarah Lin, and I am a senior at Rutgers University studying Urban Planning and Public Policy. I have been involved in efforts to combat human trafficking for a couple of years now and am grateful for every opportunity I get to use my time and resources to participate in this fight.

I first heard about sex trafficking back in middle school but never fully understood the depth or magnitude of the issue until my first semester of college. Within the first couple of weeks of my freshman year, I located and decided to join the Rutgers University chapter of International Justice Mission, a global human rights agency. Through my participation in regular IJM meetings and events, I quickly became aware of just how horrifying human trafficking is. We learned about sex trafficking busts right in my own college city, and time and time again I was stunned by the proximity of the issue as well as the reality that such a flagrant violation of human rights and dignity could be occurring right under our noses. In response, I took the time during that first semester of college to learn as much as I could about sex trafficking at the local, state, national and global levels in order to better understand what addressing this phenomenon as a college student might look like.

During my sophomore year, I joined the executive board of our Rutgers IJM chapter and worked throughout the year on different human trafficking education events and workshops, including one that I organized in the residence hall where I was living as a mentor-in-residence for first-year students. Our chapter also works closely with a local New Jersey nonprofit called Love True, an organization with a mission of fighting sex trafficking in the United States through parallel efforts in prevention education and restoration. During that same year I also applied to attend the Clinton Global Initiative University 2016 Convening in the San Francisco Bay Area. My project proposal for CGI U 2016 under the Peace and Human Rights category focused on human trafficking awareness, education and advocacy among the college student population. After returning home from an inspiring weekend at CGI U 2016, I began planning the implementation of my project on my own campus.

As a junior, I served on IJM's National Student Leadership Team alongside five other justice leaders from around the country. As the team's regional vice president of the Northeast region of the United States, I mentor, advise and act as a consultant for IJM campus chapter leaders in the Northeast, among a number of other responsibilities. This year, our team will also be traveling to Capitol Hill for a lobby and advocacy day filled with meetings in our senators' and representatives' D.C. offices. Additionally, this year has been exciting because I was able to implement most of my

CGI U project on human trafficking. Toward the end of January, Human Trafficking Awareness month, I organized Rutgers University's first Students Against Trafficking Week. I established partnerships with six student organizations that work on human trafficking and related issues, and together, our coalition of student groups co-hosted a week of awareness and education events including a film screening, educational workshop, a "Take Action" event featuring the executive director of the New Jersey Coalition Against Human Trafficking, and more. It was so amazing to see more conversations on campus happen about what exactly trafficking is and what we as college students can do to prevent and end it.

It's no surprise that human trafficking is an enormous and highly complex issue in our society. To some, the enormity and complexity of human trafficking can cause them to disengage and leave the hard, and often emotionally grueling, work to the experts. Yet I firmly believe that we all have integral roles to play in combating sex trafficking, and when we come together and fully exercise each of our talents, we can make an incredible difference.

There is an amazing network of committed students on college campuses all across the nation, and I am constantly floored by the work that fellow students are doing in response to this human rights violation. My advice for college students interested in getting involved in the fight to prevent and end sex trafficking would be to first become thoroughly educated on the issue and seek out mentors who are willing to answer questions and point you to key resources. You are always more credible and effective if your passion is grounded in facts and knowledge, and when you can intelligently communicate your convictions on this issue you care about. Next, find other individuals — perhaps students both younger and older than you — to challenge and learn with you.

Together you can identify the needs of your campus or community. Whether there's a need for more awareness, collaboration across groups, advocacy training, or more, you can take the initiative to meet these needs in robust and creative ways. Have conversations with students who have different majors and career paths, and show them how people studying medicine, information technology, law, social work, international relations, business, public policy, etc. all have critical roles to play in ending sex trafficking. As individuals in an increasingly connected society, we are well-positioned to create lasting social change that can impact the lives of millions of people facing oppression, exploitation, and horrific injustice. After I first learned about sex trafficking, I knew I could not simply avert my eyes and carry on with business as usual. I had to do something to contribute to the fight against this injustice, and I hope you and many others will join this effort, too.

Youngbee Dale
Anti-trafficking consultant
Effective Communications Strategies, LLC

Youngbee Dale

Prior to joining Effective Communications Strategies, LLC., I was a program manager at Global Centurion, the Department of Defense subject matter expert on Combating Trafficking in Persons (2013 – 2016). I also worked with trafficking victims in South Korea and the U.S., partnering with FBI agents, a senior officer at the U.S. Department of State, and various local anti-trafficking organizations.

The U.S. anti-trafficking efforts progressed tremendously since the Trafficking Victims and Protection Act came into effect in 2000. In particular, the anti-trafficking effort to combat domestic minor sex trafficking (DMST) led to several key legislations in the U.S. For instance, in 2015, President Obama signed the Justice for Victims of Trafficking Act of 2015 into law. It addresses domestic sex trafficking and the demand for DMST in the U.S. The law also provides grounds to strengthen law enforcement and increase fines for traffickers. Lastly, the law reauthorized an older provision to help DMST victims receiving federal funding for victim assistance. In 2014, the Preventing Sex Trafficking and Strengthening Families Act became a law. The legislation aimed to prevent and address the problems with DMST in the foster care system.

However, the U.S. anti-trafficking group combating foreign sex trafficking victims has not been as progressive as DMST. For instance, the anti-trafficking efforts to combat sex trafficking of Korean women in the U.S. has mainly focused on shutting down massage parlors and other storefront brothels. The exploitation of Korean women in various brothel models, parlors and other storefront brothels remains only a segment of the entire Korean commercial sex market in the U.S. In many cases, traffickers' schemes and tactics behind various brothel models have not been well known to anti-trafficking groups because of the complexity of cultural and linguistic factors.

To combat sex trafficking of Korean women more effectively, the law enforcement, NGOs and legislators must fight adjacent criminal activities supporting brothel networks as well as traffickers themselves. Some of the tactics behind brothel networks include, money laundering, tax evasion, visa fraud, corruption, or others. In particular, local law enforcement officers around the U.S. must be trained to identify these criminal activities when making prostitution-related arrests.

One recent case, *United States v. Kim et al.* (2016) demonstrates the significance of combating adjacent criminal activities. According to the complaint, Ryan Kim and his accomplice were convicted of committing money laundering after profiting from running online advertisement services for various brothels in New York. Interestingly, one of his accomplices for money laundering was located in a rural area acting as Kim's agent. The case is an example that the impact of these illegal networks affects both metropolitan and rural areas in the U.S.

The U.S. anti-trafficking groups made a significant progress in assisting domestic sex trafficking victims for the past few years. However, more work is necessary to assist foreign victims in the U.S. including those from South Korea more effectively. The U.S. anti-trafficking groups can further their efforts to combat Korean sex trafficking by arresting brothel owners as well as individuals involved in the network of brothels. The U.S. anti-trafficking efforts have made significant progress since 2000. It is vital for their effort to continue to end sex trafficking in the U.S.

SECTION VII

JOURNALISM

Lisa Driscoll
Director of FOCUS at the University of Virginia
B.A. in Journalism from the University of Maryland

Lisa Driscoll

My friend and I pulled up to a three-star hotel outside Dulles International Airport. This junction was one I frequented, due to its more affordable airfare for out-of-state students like myself. I looked over at my friend, who pulled out his camera and adjusted the lens to get a better focus, while the glare of blue and red lights shone in the rearview mirror.

We turned our gaze and watched in silence as police entered the hotel. Estimated by the illuminated room minutes later, it seemed that they had arrived on the scene. More time passed. My phone rang.

They had made an arrest, the sergeant said. This precious soul thought she was going to make money that night by selling her body to a stranger who had seen her advertisement online. Instead, it was a group of undercover police who surprised her. They said they were there to help her, and to arrest a pimp. It took some time, but she eventually admitted to having a pimp coerce her into prostitution.

He was hiding in the stairwell.

She was taken to the police station and given the opportunity for treatment and rehabilitative care, but was too shaken up for an interview.

Soon after, the police made another undercover appearance in another hotel in the same commercial district. This time, it was a friend of the officers. She went by "Jasmine" on *Backpage.com.* They had busted her several times before, but each time she said that she did not have a pimp and was willingly prostituting herself for some extra cash. Unlike the other woman, "Jasmine" was willing to have an interview.

Summoned into the hotel room, I was greeted by a young woman sitting on the bed.

I only had a couple minutes with her, so I asked some basic questions, including, "how are you?" and finally, "have you ever felt used on the job?" The latter question she spent much more time answering than the former. She was beautiful, scantily clad and seemed confident, as she smiled. She was 22, the same age as me. "Jasmine" could have been one of my classmates, for all I knew.

A couple months prior, I was just about to begin the last semester of my senior year at University of Maryland. At that point, it seemed as if my choice in classes was limited to finishing the requirements I needed to graduate on time. But in choosing a capstone class for my broadcast journalism degree, I had the unique opportunity that semester to enroll in an investigative reporting class. The topic this time was human trafficking in Maryland.

My knowledge on the scope of the problem was scant

to none at the time. I simply wanted to join a fight against the objectification of women, men and children, and this seemed to be a great way to employ my weapons of pen and paper (or, in our digital media, a keyboard and word processor).

Seasoned investigative journalists Deborah Nelson and Sandra Banisky were our editors, while our investigative journalism class reported for the Capital News Service. We gleaned through court files and public records requested through the Public Information Act by other media law and reporting classes to gather data and evidence. We also left our computers to see with our own eyes the scope of the problem, as I did with my friend that one night outside Dulles airport.

My job was to request a database with all arrests and convictions for prostitution and human trafficking from the Maryland Department of Public Safety and Correctional Services in order to get the big picture of the problem. After much communication, waiting and direction from our editors, we were able to obtain the database and compare numbers.

What we found was startling. In Maryland, human trafficking of a minor is a felony, which means serving a penalty of up to 25 years in prison upon conviction. However, trafficking an adult 18 years or older is a misdemeanor, which carries a maximum sentence of 10 years in prison. The only way an adult trafficker can be convicted with a felony is if the prosecution can prove that they used force, fraud, threat or coercion to control the victim. We saw many people who were convicted of trafficking an adult, served their sentence of a couple years, went back into trafficking, and were convicted again. It was essentially a cycle that was clearly not being stopped by the law. At the time of our reporting, a bill to strengthen penalties against adult human trafficking died in the Maryland General Assembly.

Many hours of reporting were spent staring at a database, counting numbers of convictions, fact checking and requesting public data. Yet, I couldn't forget that behind each number of cases were souls – victims of a culture of utter abuse. Human trafficking is simply a business – in fact, those who are in it call it "The Game" – in which the soul of a person is disregarded, and they become an object to prey on. For a fleeting moment, they are merely a product to give pleasure.

Yet that moment can affect both parties for a lifetime. The women we got to meet, who had either gone through rehabilitation after being trafficked or worked for organizations that provided support services, told us of the many physical and emotional scars these victims are inflicted. It can often take years for victims to heal. And even the customers – those who solicit sex, or "johns" – are still affected, whether behind physical bars of a sentence or behind the bars around their own hearts. Never was a human heart made for counterfeit love like this.

That is why it is so important for people to fight for justice for those who are trafficking others and to provide refuge and support for those who are being trafficked. As a journalist, I was always taught to be a voice for the voiceless. In the time of this reporting, I came to realize how unseen this attack on human dignity is. What we see is the tip of the iceberg, and our reporting didn't even cross state lines.

We certainly should do all we can to make human trafficking for adults in all 50 states a felony. Changing laws can help enact justice. Lawmakers, law enforcers, journalists and organizations should come together to do their part to enact change that comes from all sides of our social structure.

But to truly change the world, we must also look at our own relationships and our own culture. Do we use others purely as objects for our own enjoyment? Do we use others in a business-like transaction, as if we are in a game? Are we puritanical in our language and afraid to talk about the real meaning of sex? Do we perpetrate sex trafficking by adding to the demand, through soliciting prostitution or watching porn? If there is no demand, there is no business.

If we use our voices, let our words and actions only be ones of strength, sincerity and authentic, self-giving love.

Lisa Driscoll reported for Capital News Service investigative report, "The Brothel Next Door," published in spring 2015 (http://cnsmaryland.org/human-trafficking). After graduating from University of Maryland with degrees in broadcast journalism and vocal performance that spring, she now serves at University of Virginia for her second year of missionary work with the Fellowship of Catholic University Students.

References and Resources

Here is a list of information about the organizations that our contributors work with and/or are connected to.

Amara Legal Center

info@amaralegal.org

Provides free legal services to individuals whose rights have been violated while involved in commercial sex.

ArtWorks for Freedom

info@artworksforfreedom.org

ArtWorks for Freedom uses the power of art to raise awareness about modern day slavery and human trafficking. Working locally and globally and engaging art in all its forms, they are transforming public perceptions, educating individuals, communities and policy makers and inspiring action to put an end to modern day slavery.

Baltimore Child Abuse Center

info@bcaci.org

The mission of Baltimore Child Abuse Center is to provide victims of child sexual abuse, trauma, and other adverse childhood experiences in Baltimore and their non-offending caretakers with comprehensive forensic interviews, medical treatment and mental health treatment with a goal of preventing future trauma.

Department of Homeland Security

The Department of Homeland Security has a vital mission: to secure the nation from the many threats we face. This requires the dedication of more than 240,000 employees in jobs that range from aviation and border security to emergency response, from cyber security analyst to chemical facility inspector

FAIR Girls

info@fairgirls.org

FAIR Girls aims to prevent the exploitation of girls worldwide with empowerment and education. Through prevention education, compassionate care, and survivor inclusive advocacy, FAIR Girls creates opportunities for girls to become confident, happy, healthy young women.

Free NOLA

Free NOLA is a faith-based initiative targeting the overwhelming issue of domestic human trafficking in the New Orleans and Gulf Coast regions. Their mission is to bring awareness and stop the exploitation of men, women and children.

Governor’s Office of Crime Control and Prevention

Local governments’ one stop shop for resources to improve public safety in Maryland. The office plans, promotes, and funds efforts with government entities, private organizations, and the community to advance public policy, enhance public safety, reduce crime and juvenile delinquency, and serve victims.

Hannah’s Hope

findhope.hannah@gmail.com

Hannah's Hope is an effort dedicated to fighting human trafficking both locally and globally. Their mission is to combat this injustice by raising awareness, offering education to at risk populations, and bringing hope and restoration to those who have been affected by it.

HEAL Trafficking

healtraffickingnow@gmail.com

A united group of multidisciplinary professionals dedicated to ending human trafficking and supporting its survivors, from a public health perspective. Their mission is to mobilize a shift in the anti-trafficking paradigm toward approaches rooted in public health principles and trauma-informed care by expanding the evidence base; enhancing collaboration among multidisciplinary stakeholders; educating the broader anti-trafficking and public health community; and advocating for funding streams that enhance the public health response to trafficking.

International Justice Mission

Global organization that protects the poor from violence in the developing world.

Orphan Frontier

www.OrphanFrontier.org

Orphan Frontier is a faith based non-profit charity which exists to magnify and honor the Lord Jesus Christ by serving the spiritual and physical needs of abused and abandoned children in the U.S.A. and around the world. They promote public awareness of the vile atrocities inflicted upon children. They help to establish, sustain, advocate and raise support for projects, Christian Orphanages, Children's Homes and Children's Ministries, and the staff serving children.

The PurPLE Clinic

The PurpLE Clinic (**Purp**ose: **L**isten and **E**ngage) offers safe and sensitive health care for anyone who has experienced sexual exploitation (including sex trafficking, domestic violence, rape or abuse), selling sex or trading sex to survive.

Students Ending Slavery

umdses@gmail.com

Students Ending Slavery's mission is to raise awareness on the issue of human trafficking and to mobilize students to take part in abolishing modern-day slavery in the community, Washington, D.C., and the world through service, on-campus events, and partnerships with other campuses.

United State's Attorney's Office

The United States Attorneys serve as the nation's principal litigators under the direction of the Attorney General.

University of Maryland SAFE Center for Human Trafficking Survivors

safecenter@umd.edu

The SAFE Center provides survivor-centered and trauma-informed services that empower trafficking survivors to heal and reclaim their lives. They aim to prevent trafficking and better serve survivors through research and policy advocacy.

The Villanova Law Institute to Address Commercial Sexual Exploitation

shea.rhodes@law.villanova.edu

They educate and provide technical assistance to those who respond to commercial sexual exploitation in Pennsylvania, the United States and beyond, promoting victim-centered, trauma-informed multidisciplinary collaboration

They equip policymakers and the broader community with the skills and knowledge they need to improve the legal system's response to commercial sexual exploitation, in order to support survivors and hold perpetrators accountable.

They center the experiences of survivors to inform the development of policies and best practices to combat commercial sexual exploitation and are committed to engaging the survivor community in shaping their positions.

Willow House

Willow House at The Meadows is a 45-day inpatient program designed specifically for women who are struggling with love addiction, relationship issues and intimacy disorders.

Worthwhile Wear

Info@WorthwhileWear.org

Worthwhile Wear exists to reach and restore women affected by human trafficking, which is today's modern day slavery.

Please check out
www.BowmanPublishing.com
for more great books.

www.ingramcontent.com/pod-product-compliance
Lightning Source LLC
Chambersburg PA
CBHW060455280326
41933CB00014B/2758
* 9 7 8 0 9 9 8 8 8 6 9 1 6 *